Starting English for Business

Other ESP titles of interest include:

ADAMSON, D.
International Hotel English★

BINHAM, P. *et al.*
Hotel English★

BINHAM, P. *et al.*
Restaurant English★

BRIEGER, N. and J. Comfort
Business Contacts★

BRIEGER, N. and J. Comfort
Early Business Contacts

BRIEGER, N. and A. Cornish
Secretarial Contacts★

BRIEGER, N. and J. Comfort
Technical Contacts★

BRIEGER, N. and J. Comfort
Social Contacts★

BRIEGER, N. and J. Comfort
Business Issues

DAVIES, S. *et al.*
Bilingual Handbooks of Business Correspondence and Communication

KEANE, L.
International Restaurant English★

McGOVERN, J. and J. McGovern
Bank on Your English★

McKellen, J. and M. Spooner
New Business Matters★

PALSTRA, R.
Telephone English★

PALSTRA, R.
Telex English

POTE, M. *et al.*
A Case for Business English★

ROBERTSON, F.
Airspeak★

★ includes audio cassette(s)

Starting English for Business

DONALD ADAMSON

ENGLISH LANGUAGE TEACHING

Prentice Hall

New York London Toronto Sydney Tokyo Singapore

First published 1991 by
Prentice Hall International (UK) Ltd
66 Wood Lane End, Hemel Hempstead
Hertfordshire HP2 4RG
A division of
Simon & Schuster International Group

Typeset in 11 pt Plantin
by MHL Typesetting Ltd, Coventry

Printed in Great Britain at the University Press, Cambridge

Library of Congress Cataloging-in-Publication Data

Adamson, Donald, 1943–
    Starting English for business / Donald Adamson.
        p. cm. — (English language teaching)
    ISBN 0-13-842519-1 (International edition)
    ISBN 0-13-842592-2 (Japanese edition)
    1. English language — Textbooks for foreign speakers. 2. English
language — Business English. I. Title. II. Series.
PE1128.A33   1991
428.2'4'02465 — dc20   91-16829
                                                                  CIP

British Library Cataloguing in Publication Data

Adamson, Donald
    Starting English for business. — (English
    language teaching)
    I. Title II. Series
    428

    ISBN 0-13-842519-1 (International edition)
    ISBN 0-13-842592-2 (Japanese edition)

1 2 3 4 5   95 94 93 92 91

Contents

Introduction

The aims of the course

Starting English for Business is a pre-intermediate course for Business students who have had some basic instruction in English, but who are not — at this point — concerned with the more specialised areas of Business English.

The course aims to act as a *bridge* between general elementary material and Business English material. For this reason, it concentrates on fundamental aspects of language — functions, structures and other areas — within business contexts. In so doing it aims to pave the way for more specialised materials involving case studies, simulations and so on.

Along with the teaching and practice of necessary language and functions, the course aims to help students and instructors in diagnosing problem areas which practice can help to put right.

The level of the course

The course can be used by students of various levels, as follows:

- At its lowest level, the course can be used selectively to follow on an intensive beginners' course. In this situation, units could be chosen by the teacher for practice of points already covered, but within more business-related situations, and providing basic business vocabulary.

- More typically, the course will be used following one or two years of general instruction up to elementary level, as a means of reviewing basic language, practising some business-related functions and in general preparing for more specialised Business English teaching.

- The material will also be useful to the 'false beginner' — the student who has picked up English in a haphazard way from earlier instruction, but whose absorption of the language is unsystematic and full of errors. The course will give the students an opportunity to review earlier teaching and to see what they know, or don't know. It will give them another chance to look at basic points in an organised way, within business contexts.

- At higher levels, even with students who are capable of tackling more advanced Business English, the course may be useful in providing review material, allowing students to refine and perfect knowledge in areas where they still show weaknesses.

The components of the course

The course components are:

- The Student's Book, containing the main 'language in use' units, a section on Business Correspondence, the Information Gap section, the Tapescript, the Answer Key and a Word List

- A C60 cassette. The taped material is an integral part of the course. It contains material for the initial listening tasks, and also material for stress and intonation practice.

Modular nature of the course

The main units (Units 1–24) are laid out according to modular principles. There is no 'story line' and no need for users to follow the order of units given. Units can be picked out according to the needs of the students.

Nevertheless, the order of the units as given has been decided so that instructors who wish to follow the book right through can do so with confidence. Units are ordered so that a greater range of grammar structures appears in the book as it progresses. Although totally rigid structural grading is not a feature, simplicity has required the avoidance of too many 'new' structures in any given unit. A degree of structural control is seen as useful.

The content of units

In deciding on the focus of the units, several elements contribute, with different elements uppermost in different units, as follows:

1 *A 'notional' component.* Certain notions such as 'time', 'number' and 'quantity' are fundamental to business interactions as well as having direct implications for the grammar and functions covered.

2 *A grammatical/structural component.* One aim of the course is to review important grammar points within business contexts. Thus in the course of the twenty-four units there is practice of important areas of grammar. Whenever possible, the grammar is linked to particular 'functions', see below.

3 *A 'functional' component.* Functions such as reporting, forecasting and comparing are fundamental to business and also have a direct relationship with grammar (past and future tenses and comparative forms). Other functions such as greeting and making polite conversation are also important for business, but are related to patterns of social interaction rather than to particular grammatical forms. The more interaction-related functions appear towards the end of the book — but of course the instructor is at liberty to cover them at any time.

4 *A 'utilities' component.* It is important for the student to be able to say numbers and times correctly, to use letters of the alphabet to give abbreviations and to spell out words, to know how to talk about countries of origin, and so on. Units practising these 'utilities' occur from time to time in the course of the book.

5 *Vocabulary.* Words and expressions related to business are brought in as necessary, often with repetition from unit to unit. However, the aim is to avoid too much new vocabulary in any one unit. A word list is included at the end of the book.

Unit structure

Units 1–24 are divided up as follows:

1 *Listening focus.* Each unit begins with listening activities. The listening input (conversations or a short passage) is designed to present the language focused on within the unit. The listening tasks typically involve (a) extracting and noting down some simple information (so that the student's mind is 'set' towards deriving information from particular forms); (b) focusing directly on the form itself, isolating it from the stream of language heard on the tape.

Notice that this section does not set out to practise highly sophisticated listening skills through complex inputs. The tasks are pitched so as to introduce particular forms and functions in a simple, approachable manner.

2 *Controlled practice.* This provides simple written exercises to practise the language focused on in the unit. The formats are designed to be self-evident (e.g. sentence completion, transformation, matching).

3 *Activity.* This section provides tasks of a more open-ended nature, often involving pair or group work. Sometimes there is an 'Information gap exercise', with Student A having access to different information from Student B. (Students question each

other to complete the task.) Sometimes the task is a project, requiring students to collect information from their own environment and to report back.

4   *Language reference.*   This is a resource section which can be used by students and instructors as required. Students at truly elementary levels will obviously need help in understanding the explanations — explanations which the instructor may or may not decide to give in a particular teaching situation. Students at higher levels may be able to study the explanations for themselves.

   The explanations have been kept as short as possible, and the 'facts' have been simplified. These simplifications have been arrived at through considerable thought and discussion, but experience shows that no two individuals will agree on what facts are necessary, or on what is 'simple'. Instructors are therefore invited to adapt the explanations to their own classroom situation.

Self-study

Much of the material is designed to be suitable for students working on their own. The Listening focus and Controlled practice sections are both eminently suitable as self-access material, with students referring to the Answer Key as necessary. The Language reference section can also be read by students above the very lowest level. Even many of the Activity sections could be undertaken by students working in pairs, with minimal control by the instructor.

The author and publishers welcome comments from users. Comments should be sent to The Managing Editor (ELT), Prentice Hall International, Hemel Hempstead, Herts, United Kingdom.

To the instructor

Starting English for Business can be used with students at various levels. However, it is important to approach the course in ways most suitable to the level. Here are some hints on using the course:

1 The course aims to include a good deal of basic business vocabulary. For students at the lowest level, unfamiliar vocabulary could make the course seem difficult. If you are teaching elementary students, you will need to do some pre-teaching of vocabulary.

   Check through units before you use them in class, and make a list of words which you think will be unfamiliar to your students. It is best if students can be encouraged to GUESS the meaning of words from the surrounding sentence, but if you really think the load of new words is too high, put some words on the board before the lesson begins. You can get students to look the words up and discuss their meanings. Try to elicit sentences in which the words might be used. This will be good preparation for the Listening and Controlled practice sections.

2 A similar commonsense approach applies to the opening Listening focus tasks. Normally, students first indicate meanings (comprehension), THEN focus on the actual forms which express the meanings. However, with very weak students you could decide to do things THE OTHER WAY ROUND. If you feel that your students can only get at the meaning by picking out the actual forms first, switch tasks round so that students go first to the actual words used in the conversations. (But remember that the long-term aim should be to get students to deal with meanings, not to get trapped in word-by-word comprehension.)

3 Be flexible in the way you play recorded conversations. Normally you will play complete dialogues through once or twice to begin with (for general comprehension), but remember that you can always stop the tape and introduce pauses to allow students to 'catch up'. You can also stop the tape and get students to repeat sentences as you wish.

4   Adapt the Activity section to suit your classroom circumstances, taking into account age, student expectations and learning styles. In some classes the atmosphere will be informal, and group and pair work will come naturally, without too much intervention from the instructor. In other classes a more structured approach may be preferred, with exemplification and illustration from selected students, pairs in front of the class, and so on.

5   Adapt the Language reference explanations according to the level and mother tongue of the students. If experience tells you that certain explanations 'work' in your country, use them.

6   Be ready to supplement the Activity work with any suitable tasks of your own devising. (Indeed the same applies to all the tasks in the course, for example to the suggestions on subjects for letters in the Business Correspondence section.)

7   Although rote-learning is not an end in itself (and is sometimes regarded as incompatible with 'communicative' teaching), it may be helpful to students to learn by heart items of business vocabulary, some sections of the dialogues and — definitely — correspondence formats.

8   At all levels, try to say as little as possible yourself and to get your students to say as much as possible. Avoid instant correction of students' answers. Be silent, giving students time to monitor their output and correct themselves, or correct each other.

Acknowledgements

The author is grateful to the following advisers whose reports enabled the material to reach its present form:

Nancy Baxer, Prentice Hall Regents, Japan
Nick Brieger and Jeremy Comfort, York Associates, UK
Dan Cotterall-Debay and Diane Legree, Kiwi English Consultants, France
Susan Garvin, British Institute of Florence, Italy
Ann Laws, Linguarama, UK
Michael Sorey, Department of Human Resources, American Insurance Underwriters, Tokyo, Japan
Sylvia Welycko, Freelance Consultant, UK

The author also wishes to thank Fisher Duncan Editorial and Production Services for expert help and advice, and Isobel Fletcher de Téllez for her varied work on this book.

UNIT 1

Places of origin

(nationality words; present tense of *be*)

1 Listening focus

Listen. Fill in the blanks with the correct countries from this list.

India Germany Switzerland Australia Britain Russia Spain
France Italy Japan Taiwan America Poland Korea

1

3

5

2

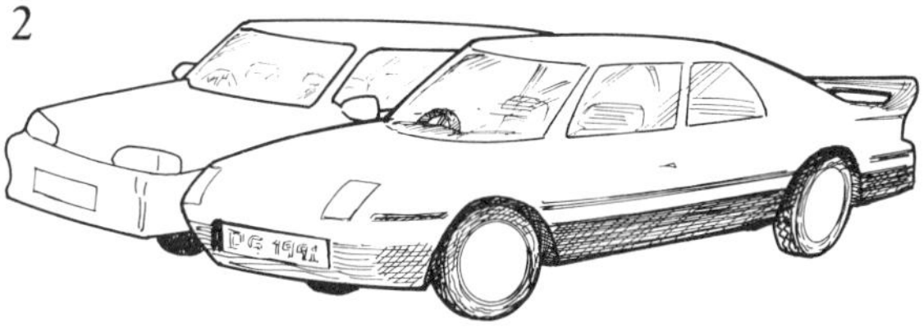

4

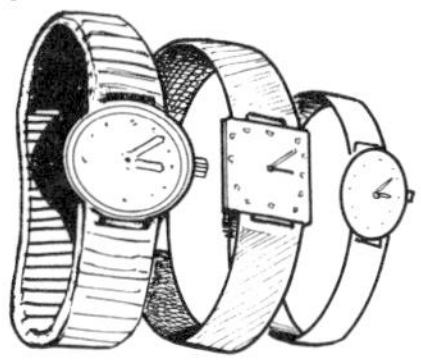

6

1. MADE IN ______ 2. *Made in* ______ 3. **Made in** ______

4. Made in ______ 5. Made in ______ 6. *Made in* ______

2 Controlled practice

2.1 *Origins and nationalities.* Here are some of the people at a conference, and the countries they come from.

Participants

Mr Al Arabi	Egypt
Professor Banda	Kenya
Mrs Delgado	Spain
Miss Dupont	France
Ann and Rita Lam	Malaysia
Tom and Peter Ho	China
Mr Larssen	Sweden
Miss Lehtonen	Finland
Mr and Mrs Moran	Ireland
Dr Muller	Germany
Mr and Mrs Rose	Australia
Mr Schultz	Canada

Look at these questions and answers:

Where is Mr Larssen from?
He's from Sweden. He's Swedish.

Answer these questions in the same way. Use the Language reference section if necessary.

1 Where is Miss Dupont from?
2 Where is Mrs Delgado from?
3 Where are Mr and Mrs Rose from?
4 Where are Tom and Peter Ho from?

Ask and answer in the same way about other people in the list. Then WRITE four questions and answers.

2.2 Look at these questions and answers:

Is Mr Larssen Swedish?
Yes, he's Swedish.
Is Miss Dupont Dutch?
No, she isn't Dutch. She's French.

Answer the questions below. Then ask and answer in the same way about other people in the list. WRITE four questions and answers.

1 Is Miss Lehtonen Danish?
2 Are Ann and Rita Lam Malaysian?
3 Is Dr Müller German?
4 Are Mr and Mrs Moran English?

2.3 Answer this question for Miss Dupont:

Where are you from?

And this question for Mrs Delgado:

Are you Italian?

And these questions for YOURSELF:

Where are you from?
Are you English?

2.4 Here are some more people at the conference. Where are they from? What nationality are they? Unscramble the letters as in 1 and 2.

1 Mr and Mrs Cobb are from WEN EAZANDL.   _N E W   Z E A L A N D_

2 Professor Nadu is NIDINA.   _I N D I A N_

3 Dr Alemao is RTUGSEEOUP.   _ _ _ _ _ _ _ _ _ _

4 Miss Samson is from HTE SUA.   _ _ _   _ _ _ _

5 Mr Olsen is from MARKNDE.   _ _ _ _ _ _ _

6 Mr Van Rijk is DHCTU.   _ _ _ _ _

7 Mr Hajjaj is from DISAU ABIARA.   _ _ _ _ _   _ _ _ _ _ _

8 Dr Intissar is from ANTISPAK.   _ _ _ _ _ _ _ _

9 Mr and Mrs Lobo are TINIANENARG.   _ _ _ _ _ _ _ _ _ _ _

10 Mr Atmaca is from YEKUTR.   _ _ _ _ _ _

3 Activity

3.1 Talk about things you have, and their place of origin. For example:

My car is (German).
My shoes are (Italian).

3.2 Find out about the nationality of some big companies in your country. Talk about them to your class. For example:

(MacDonalds) is an (American) company.

3.3 In a group, discuss and make a list of people you know in your class or your company who come from different countries. Write name tags that they could wear at a conference (or wear in your class — if you are from different countries).

4 Language reference

Countries; with adjectives

Adjectives ending in *-an* (the most common type)

Algeria — Algerian	America (the USA) — American
Russia (the USSR) — Russian	Australia — Australian
Malaysia — Malaysian	Indonesia — Indonesian
India — Indian	Germany — German
Italy — Italian	Korea — Korean
Norway — Norwegian	Brazil — Brazilian
Egypt — Egyptian	Argentina — Argentinian
Belgium — Belgian	Canada — Canadian
Kenya — Kenyan	Nigeria — Nigerian

Adjectives ending in *-ese*

Japan — Japanese	China — Chinese
Portugal — Portuguese	Vietnam — Vietnamese
Taiwan — Taiwanese	

Adjectives ending in *-ish*

Britain (the UK) — British	Finland — Finnish
Poland — Polish	Sweden — Swedish
Spain — Spanish	Denmark — Danish
Turkey — Turkish	

Adjectives ending in *-i*

Pakistan — Pakistani	Saudi Arabia — Saudi
	(but you can also use Saudi Arabi*an*)

Others

France — French	The Netherlands - Dutch
Switzerland — Swiss	Greece — Greek
The Philippines — Philippine	Hong Kong — Hong Kong
New Zealand — New Zealand	(no change)
(no change)	

Present tense of *be*

Positive statements

I'm He's/She's/It's We're/You're/They're	Italian.

In formal writing: *I am*
       He is, etc.
       We are, etc.

Questions

Is he/she/it Are you/they	Italian?

Negative statements

I'm not He/She/It isn't We/You/They aren't	Italian.

We CANNOT say 'I amn't'

Use of indefinite article (*a/an***)**

Use *a/an* when you first mention something that is singular and countable:
 It's *a* German car. It's *an* Italian refrigerator.

DO NOT use *a/an* with words that are plural or uncountable:
 They're German cars. (*cars* is plural)
 It's Spanish wine. (*wine* is uncountable)

Numbers (1): Basic inquiries and information

(numbers 1−100; *there is/are; have*)

1 Listening focus

A business tycoon is planning a takeover. Listen to the conversation about two firms, Axon and Bentel. At the top of the next page there is a table. Fill in the missing headings (a) and (b), and the missing numbers (c)−(h).

	Axon	**Bentel**
New products	(c) _____	(f) _____
(a) _____	(d) _____	150
(b) _____	17	(g) _____
Market share	(e) _____ %	(h) _____ %

2   Controlled practice

In a warehouse. John is a driver. Mick is a warehouse assistant. Complete the conversation below. Use any suitable phrases from this list (usually more than one answer is possible). Begin with a capital letter if necessary.

I have	we have	do you have
are there	do we have	he has
there aren't	you have	is there
there are	there's	

JOHN: How many loads ^{1}_____ for me today?
MICK: ^{2}_____ eight loads to deliver — five small ones and three large ones.
JOHN: Are they packed?
MICK: No, we'll have to pack them.
JOHN: What about crates? ^{3}_____ enough?
MICK: ^{4}_____ twenty small crates here. But ^{5}_____ enough large crates. In fact, ^{6}_____ only one large crate left.
JOHN: I'll phone the Transport Manager at the factory. Sometimes ^{7}_____ crates.

(on the telephone to the Transport Manager)

JOHN: Hello. This is John at the warehouse. ^{8}_____ any large crates? ^{9}_____ some big loads to deliver.
TRANSPORT MANAGER: ^{10}_____ two large crates here. Come and get them.
JOHN: ^{11}_____ anyone to help me lift them? I can't lift them myself.
TRANSPORT MANAGER: ^{12}_____ six men here. They'll help you.

3 Activity

3.1 Say numbers between 1 and 1000 to your partner. Take a note of the numbers. Your partner writes the numbers down. Then check your partner's answers.

Include some numbers that are difficult to hear clearly, for example:

13 and 30 (and similarly 113 and 130, 213 and 230, etc.)
14 and 40
15 and 50
(and so on)

3.2 Find out about your firm, or any firm in your country. Answer questions about numbers and percentages, like those below. Report to the rest of your class.

How many	employees branches divisions sales outlets factories etc.	does it have?

What percentage of the workforce	are manual workers? are office workers? etc.

How many products does it have in its catalogue?
What percentage of the market does it have?

4   Language reference

Saying or writing out numbers 1–1000: examples:

0 zero or 'oh'	13 thirteen	20 twenty	30 thirty
1 one	14 fourteen	21 twenty-one	40 forty
2 two	15 fifteen	22 twenty-two	50 fifty
3 three	16 sixteen	23 twenty-three	60 sixty
4 four	17 seventeen	24 twenty-four	70 seventy
5 five	18 eighteen	25 twenty-five	80 eighty
6 six	19 nineteen	26 twenty-six	90 ninety
7 seven		27 twenty-seven	
8 eight		28 twenty-eight	
9 nine		29 twenty-nine	
10 ten			
11 eleven			
12 twelve			

100 a hundred (OR one hundred)
101 a hundred and one (OR one hundred and one, etc.)
110 a hundred and ten
199 a hundred and ninety-nine
200 two hundred
999 nine hundred and ninety-nine
1000 a thousand (OR one thousand)

Notes:
1 American English: *a hundred ninety-nine*, etc. (missing out *and*)
2 Percentages: the % sign is read as *per cent*, for example:
    25% = twenty-five per cent.

Forms of *have*

Questions

How many employees	do I/you/we/they does he/she/it	have?

Positive statements

I/you/we/they have He/she/it has	200 employees.

Note: In British English we use *have got* as well as *have* (see Unit 10):

> How many computers *have you got?*
> *We've got* twenty computers.

Have got is used more with objects that can be moved around.

> How many chairs *have we got?*

Have is used more with 'permanent' possessions, and with people.

> *We have* 200 employees.

But both forms are usually correct.

There is/There are

Questions

	Is there	a photocopier in this office?
How many messages	are there	for me?

Positive statements

There's   one photocopier. There are   three messages.

There's (speech) = *There is* (writing)

Negative statements

There isn't   time. There aren't   any messages.

There isn't (speech) = *There is not* (writing)
There aren't (speech) = *there are not* (writing)

UNIT 3

Basic descriptions

(simple present tense: questions, statements and negative forms)

1 Listening focus

1.1 *Describing a firm.* Listen to questions and answers about Extel. Complete rows 2—5 in the table opposite.

1 Goods manufactured	*microcomputers, word processors*
2 Countries sold to	
3 Type of market	
4 Number of workers	
5 Yearly sales	
6 Type of training	
7 Own microprocessors?	(Yes/No)

1.2   Listen to more questions and answers. Fill in the missing words.

Question: _____ _____ of _____ _____ you _____ your
workers?
Answer: Every employee _____ basic _____ on the job.
Some _____ _____ day-release _____.

Question: _____ the company _____ its own microprocessors?
Answer: _____, we _____ _____ our own microprocessors.
We _____ them from _____.

Now write answers for rows 6 and 7 in the table.

2   Controlled practice

2.1   *Describing a course.* Read the conversation. Then write the correct form of the verbs in italics (the first is done for you). Some verbs become QUESTIONS, some become NEGATIVE forms, and some DO NOT CHANGE. If there is no change, put a dash (—).

JOHN: Is it a long course? How long [1]*it lasts*?
TOMIKO: Oh, [2]*my course lasts* very long — only one year. But [3]*some courses last* two or three years. [4]*A lot of students continue* at higher levels.
JOHN: What subjects [5]*you study*?
TOMIKO: Well, [6]*every student studies* accountancy, office practice and business administration. And [7]*we choose* other subjects, according to our interests.

JOHN: What qualification [8]*you get* at the end of the course? [9]*You get* a Master's degree?

TOMIKO: Oh no. [10]*We get* a Master's degree from a short course — just a Diploma.

JOHN: [11]*The training involves* spending some time with a firm?

TOMIKO: Yes. [12]*Every student spends* some time with a firm. [13]*The firm writes* a report on us. [14]*The report helps* to decide our grade at the end of the course.

1 *does it last* _____   8 _____
2 _____   9 _____
3 _____   10 _____
4 _____   11 _____
5 _____   12 _____
6 _____   13 _____
7 _____   14 _____

2.2   *Describing a country.* Read this passage.

[1]Atlantis has important oil reserves. [2]It produces more oil than any other country in the region. [3]In fact, it exports oil throughout the world.

[4]The factories of Atlantis manufacture plastic goods and other petroleum-based products.

[5]Atlantis does not have a large agricultural sector. [6]It imports nearly all the food it needs.

From the notes below, write questions which are answered in the passage. Which sentences in the passage do the questions refer to?

(a) oil / how much / Atlantis / produce / does

_____ Sentence _____

(b) natural resources / have / does / Atlantis / what

_____ Sentence _____

(c) does / manufacture / what kind of / goods / Atlantis

_____ Sentence _____

(d) food / does / how much / import / it

_____ Sentence _____

(e) Atlantis / much agriculture / have / does

_____ Sentence _____

3 Activity

3.1   Find out about a company in your country. Find answers to questions like these:

What does it do?
What goods or services does it provide?
Where does it sell its goods or its services?
Who does it belong to?
How much profit does it make?
How much does it pay its employees?

Then work in pairs and take parts as below.

Student A
You meet B at a conference. You want to know about B's company. Ask questions about B's company. Answer questions about YOUR company.

Student B
You meet A at a conference. He/she asks you about your company. Be ready to answer questions. Ask A questions about his/her company.

Which company would you prefer to work for?

3.2   Find out about a country in your part of the world. Collect a few facts about its economic activity (what it produces, what it exports, what it imports, and so on). Prepare a short report (spoken or written).

Try to answer questions asked by your instructor or by other students.

3.3   Describe a company or country WITHOUT GIVING ITS NAME. Other students try to guess the company or country you are talking about.

4 Language reference

Descriptions often use the simple present tense, as follows:

Positive statements

I/you/we/they produce He/she/it produces	high-quality goods.

Questions

The main question forms contain *do* or *does*.

(1)	What kind of goods	do you/we/they does he/she/it	produce?	
	(2)	Do you/we/they Does he/she/it	produce	high-quality goods?

Note: The first type of question is a *Wh*-question (it begins with a question word). The second is a *yes/no* question (it needs the answer *yes* or *no*). The verb form is the same in both types of question.

Negative statements

Negative forms contain *don't* (= *do not*) or *doesn't* (= *does not*).

I/you/we/they don't He/she/it doesn't	produce	enough high-quality goods.

Note: *Don't* and *doesn't* are used in conversation. *Do not* and *does not* are used in formal writing (e.g. business letters and reports).

UNIT 4

Letters and abbreviations

(saying letters and abbreviations; spelling out names)

1 Listening focus

1.1 Listen. Write the names you hear.

1 _____   4 _____
2 _____   5 _____
3 _____

1.2 Listen. Match the conversations with the phrases.

Conversation 1 _____   (a)   International Telephone and Telegraph Corporation
Conservation 2 _____   (b)   Greenwich Mean Time
Conservation 3 _____   (c)   video cassette recorder
Conservation 4 _____   (d)   polyvinyl chloride
Conversation 5 _____   (e)   cash on delivery

2 Controlled practice

2.1   Complete the sentences below with abbreviations from these phrases.

European Economic Community   Visual display unit
Postscript (= something you add at the   Financial Times
   end of a letter, after your name)   Sale or return
International Monetary Fund   Do It Yourself
Value Added Tax   Imperial Chemical Industries
Annual General Meeting   British Broadcasting Corporation

1   This is the _____ World Service. Here is the news.
2   This computer costs £399 plus _____ at $17\frac{1}{2}$ per cent.
3   Nowadays people have more time to do jobs around the house, so the market
     for _____ goods is expanding.
4   Harry's letter has a _____. He sends his best wishes to everyone in the office.
5   The _____ has an interesting article today about the Japanese economy.
6   _____ is one of the largest companies in the United Kingdom.
7   A lot of countries obtain loans from the _____.
8   France and Germany are important members of the _____.
9   Most office workers don't like to stare at a _____ all day.
10 We supply the goods on an _____ basis — if you don't sell them, you can
     send them back to us.
11 Our company has its _____ next month.

3 Activity

3.1   Read out these abbreviations. How many of them do you know? Work with other
students and find out what the letters stand for.

(used in education) MA, BComm, ESL, IQ
(used in writing letters) sae, c/o, PTO
(names of countries) USA, USSR, GB
(names of international organisations) UN, WHO
(used in agreements to supply goods) FAS, FOB, CIF, C&F
(names of companies) GM, IBM, NCR, BP, TWA
(used for jobs in companies) MD, PA, CEO
(someone you must treat with great respect) VIP

3.2   Make a list of abbreviations which are common in your business. Read them out
to other students. See if they know what the letters stand for.

3.3 Practise spelling names to your partner (e.g. your name, the name of your boss, the name of your company). Check what your partner writes down.

4 Language reference

The letters and their sounds

	With an 'ee' sound as in 'see'	With an 'e' sound as in 'men'	With an 'ay' sound as in 'pay'	Other
A			A	
B	B			
C	C			
D	D			
E	E			
F		F		
G	G			
H			H	
I				I (like 'eye')
J			J	
K			K	
L		L		
M		M		
N		N		
O				O (rhymes with 'go')
P	P			
Q				Q (rhymes with 'do')
R				R (rhymes with 'car')
S		S		
T	T			
U				U (like 'you')
V	V			
W				W (double U)
X		X		
Y				Y (like 'why')
Z	Z (American)	Z (British)		

Note: Z is pronounced 'zed' in British English, and 'zee' in American English.

Numbers (2): Specifying measurements

(decimal numbers; dimension adjectives and nouns; measurements)

1 Listening focus

1.1 Listen to the conversations.
Fill in the measurements.

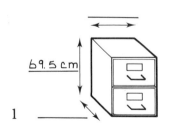

1 _____

69.5 cm

2 _____

1.5 m

3 _____

2.2 m

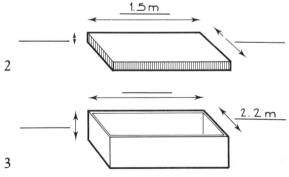

1.2 Fill in this table of 'measurement' words. All the words are in the conversations.

Noun	Adjective
height	
	deep
	wide
	long
thickness	

1.3 Listen again to part of Conversation 2. Fill in these questions and answers about WEIGHT.

A: And the _____ of each panel? What do they _____ ?
B: They're quite _____ . Each panel _____ 22.5 kilos.

2 Controlled practice

Fill in the conversations about the objects on the right.

1
A: What's the _____ of the fridge?
B: It's 85 centimetres _____ . The _____ is 52 centimetres and the _____ of the shelves is 48.5 centimetres.

2
A: Can you give me the measurements? How _____ is it?
B: It's 0.75 metres wide.
A: And the _____ ?
B: 1.96 metres.
A: And the _____ ?
B: It's 3.7 centimetres _____ .

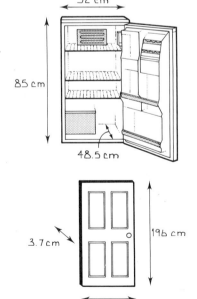

3
A: What are the dimensions of the
   package?
B: It's about 40 centimetres _____ ,
   30 centimetres _____ and 16
   centimetres _____ .
A: I see. And what does it _____ ?
B: It _____ about 10 kilos.

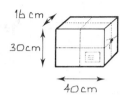

3   Activity

3.1   What measurements (height, width, etc.) would you mention in an advertisement for these objects? Discuss.

> a car, a room for rent, bookshelves, a cupboard, a set of encyclopaedias, a writing desk, a water tank, a dishwasher, a pair of binoculars, a TV set, a fishing rod, a pocket calculator, a bonsai tree

3.2   Find advertisements giving dimensions and weights (e.g. mail-order advertisements for cameras, personal stereos). Put the advertisements on display so that other students can see them. Discuss the goods — do they offer good value for money?

3.3   Imagine that you want to sell something you own (e.g. a radio, a microwave oven, a car), or something in your classroom (e.g. a piece of furniture). Write an advertisement giving specifications of the goods (e.g. dimensions, weight, selling price). Make measurements if necessary.

Put your advertisement on the wall, along with other advertisements. Look at the advertisements. Decide which goods you would like to buy.

3.4   *Information gap exercise.*   Work in pairs. Student A looks at the information below. Student B looks at the information on page 137.

Student A
You are going on holiday with Student B. You need a camera to take with you. Obtain information about camera B. Answer questions about camera A.

The cameras have the same features — lenses, speeds, etc. Which camera offers better value for money?

Camera A		Camera B

Width:	12.4 cm
Height:	6.5 cm
Depth:	5.3 cm
Weight:	250 gm
Price:	£72

Camera B

Dimensions: _____

_____

_____

Weight: _____

Price: _____

4 Language reference

Decimal numbers: examples

1.1 = one point one
1.25 = one point two five (NOT 'one point twenty-five')
1.375 = one point three seven five
1.01 = one point oh one
0.5 = oh point five

Structures of measurement

	Adjectives			Nouns
How	long	is it?	What's its	length?
	wide			width?
	high			height?
	thick			thickness?
	deep			depth?

	Adjectives			Nouns	
It's 10 centimetres	long.		The	length	is 10 centimetres.
	wide.			width	
	high.			height	
	thick.			thickness	
	deep.			depth	

Notes:
Use *high/height* for 'upward' (vertical, 'into the air') measurements.
Use *long/length* when the main measurement is 'along the ground' (horizontal).
Use *thick/thickness* when one dimension is very small (often with solid objects).
Use *deep/depth* for objects you can look into, from the front to the back of an object.
Use *wide/width* for the measurement from one side to another.

Often we don't use 'dimension' words. We just say *by*:

33 × 24 × 10 cm = 'thirty-three *by* twenty four *by* ten centimetres'

Talking about weight

How heavy is it?	(notice the adjective *heavy*)
What does it weigh?	(notice the verb *weigh*)
What's the weight?	(notice the noun *weight*)
It weighs 10 kilograms.	(notice the verb *weigh*)
The weight is 10 kilograms.	(notice the noun *weight*)

Time (1): Schedules and timetables

(times and time expressions; simple present for scheduled events)

1   Listening focus

1.1   *Scheduled future events*. Listen to a manager discussing her programme for tomorrow. Fill in the times at which events happen.

<table>
<tr><td colspan="2">7 Tuesday</td></tr>
<tr><td>Briefing for new PAs</td><td>8.30 a.m.</td></tr>
<tr><td>Planning session</td><td>9.00</td></tr>
<tr><td>Meeting Mr. Black (Itemco)</td><td>_____</td></tr>
<tr><td>Lunch, Tec-2000 Exhibition</td><td>_____</td></tr>
<tr><td>Go round Tec-2000 Exhibition</td><td>_____</td></tr>
<tr><td>Arrival MD, Mercury Robotics</td><td>_____</td></tr>
</table>

1.2   Listen again. Complete the sentences spoken by the secretary, below.

1 _____ the planning session you _____ the new PAs.
2 They _____ work tomorrow and you _____ them a briefing.
3 Then we _____ the planning session.
4 The session _____ _____ quarter to eleven.
5 _____ _____ you _____ a meeting with Mr Black of Itemco, _____
   eleven _____ twelve.
6 You _____ to the Tec-2000 Exhibition and _____ lunch there.
7 The exhibition _____ _____ _____ half past three.
8 The Managing Director of Mercury Robotics _____ tomorrow.

2   Controlled practice

2.1   Write the correct times in the blanks using numbers with *a.m.* and *p.m.*

1

(in the afternoon)

_____

2

(in the morning)

_____

3

_____

4

FLIGHT BA 162 LEAVES AT NINETEEN TWENTY-FIVE HOURS

_____

5

(in the evening)

_____

6

THE BUSINESS WOMAN OF THE YEAR AWARDS ARE AT HALF PAST NINE TONIGHT.

_____

2.2 *Regular events*. Martin is a student at Richman Business College. Look at his timetable.

10.30 - 11.40	*Business Administration (lecture)*
11.40 - 11.45	*Break*
11.45 - 12.30	*Finance Planning (Workshop)*
12.30 - 14.00	*Lunch*
14.00 - 15.30	*Politics/economics (seminar)*
15.30 -	*Private study*

Now complete the description of his day at the college, below. Use the following words:

about	after($\times 2$)	at	before	begin	begins	between
continue	ends	from	goes	have($\times 2$)	spend	till($\times 2$)

'The course <u> 1 </u> at ten thirty. We <u> 2 </u> with a lecture on Business Administration and <u> 3 </u> with a workshop on Financial Planning <u> 4 </u> eleven forty-five. There's a five-minute break <u> 5 </u> the workshop.

The workshop <u> 6 </u> on <u> 7 </u> twelve thirty. <u> 8 </u> that we <u> 9 </u> a break for lunch. That's <u> 10 </u> half past twelve and two.

Our afternoon classes last <u> 11 </u> two o'clock <u> 12 </u> three thirty. We <u> 13 </u> a seminar on Politics and Economics.

<u> 14 </u> the classes I usually <u> 15 </u> an hour on private study or homework. So it's usually <u> 16 </u> four thirty when my day at the college <u> 17 </u> .'

3 Activity

3.1 Think of times that are important in the day. For example:

- The time when work begins
- The time when you have your lunch
- The best time to talk to your Department Manager
- The best time to phone you in the office, etc.

Now work with a partner. Practise SAYING times. You can also practise WRITING times, like this:

Student A
Make sentences about times using a mixture of forms *to* and *past*, *a.m.* and *p.m.* For example:

Work begins at half past eight.
OR Work begins at eight thirty a.m.

Student B
Write the times in the 24-hour form (e.g. 0830, 1645)

Students A and B
Check answers, then switch parts round.

3.2 Work with a partner — someone you don't know well. Try to get to know your partner by asking about his/her daily routine.

When What time	do you	go ...? have ...? etc.
How long does ... last?		

3.3 *Information gap.*   Work with a partner. Student A follows the instructions below. Student B follows the instructions on page 137.

Student A
You are Student B's secretary. You have a list in your desk diary of B's engagements and appointments for a day in the future (see opposite).
Student B also has a list in his/her personal diary. Unfortunately, some of the details on the two lists do not match!

Discuss the times and people on the lists with Student B. Work out the differences between the two lists.
With Student B, decide on the most suitable times and make suggestions (e.g. about rescheduling an appointment, etc.). For example, you could say:

'Perhaps we can change the (appointment) to ... (new time).'
'Perhaps you can (have lunch) between ... and ... (new times).'

19 Friday

9   9.30 – 10.30   Reports to write
           NO INTERRUPTIONS !!

10   10. 40 – 12. 00
      Meeting (Gloria Fox, Femina Fashions)
11

12 noon   12. 15 – 2. 00
      Lunch with John Borman, Systems Analyst
1 pm

2   2. 00 – 3. 30
      Give audiovisual presentation (sales)

3   3.40 – 5. 00
      Meet MD (about new advertising campaign)
4

5   5. 15 Cocktails (visiting VIPs from Japan)

4   Language reference

Ways of writing and saying times

In business, we often WRITE times using *a.m.* and *p.m.* We can SAY *a.m.* and *p.m.*
OR *in the morning, in the afternoon, in the evening, at night*:

     5.00 a.m. = 'five ay-em'   (OR five in the morning)
     2.00 p.m. = 'two pee-em'   (OR two in the afternoon)
     6.30 p.m. = 'six thirty pee-em'   (OR six thirty in the evening)
     9.45 p.m. = 'nine forty-five pee-em'   (OR nine forty-five at night)

We often say times on the hour using *o'clock*. We can add *in the morning*, etc:

> six o'clock (in the morning)
> eleven o'clock (at night)

In everyday conversations we can say *ten past, half past, twenty to*, etc:

> 10.05 = five past ten (Americans may say *five after ten*)
> 10.15 = (a) quarter past ten (we can miss out *a*)
> 10.30 = half past ten
> 10.40 = twenty to eleven (Americans may say *twenty of eleven*)
> 10.45 = (a) quarter to eleven.

We often use *about*, like this:

> 10.04/10.06 = It's about five past ten.

For airport or train times, radio broadcasts, etc. we can use the twenty-four-hour clock:

> 0100 hrs = 'oh one hundred (hours)'   1200 hrs = 'twelve hundred (hours)'
> 0130 hrs = 'oh one thirty (hours)'   1815 hrs = 'eighteen fifteen (hours)'

Notice common ways of saying these times:

> 1200 hrs = midday   OR   twelve noon
> 2400 hrs = midnight   OR   twelve o'clock at night

Giving information about schedules and timetables

For events in a regular timetable we use the simple present tense:

> On Tuesdays *we have* a lecture on Business Administration.
> When *do our classes finish* today?

We can use the simple present to talk about the FUTURE, as part of a definite timetable. This often happens with the verbs *have, is/are, arrive, start, finish*:

> You *have* a meeting with Dr Fisher tomorrow.
> The Board Meeting *is* at three o'clock this afternoon.
> The new Sales Manager *starts* work next week.

Some common expressions with times:

> *at* ten o'clock
> *from* eleven *till* twelve
> *between* twelve *and* one
> *after* (*After* that ..., *After* the meeting ..., etc.)
> *before* (*Before* that ..., *Before* lunch ..., etc.)

UNIT 7

The current situation

(present continuous for actions now; telephoning; refusing; excusing)

1   Listening focus

1.1   Listen. Read the actions in the table. Write a tick (✓) if they ARE happening. Write a cross (✗) if they are NOT happening. The first one is done for you.

Writing a report	✗	Showing visitors round	
Writing an article		Winning a lot of orders	
Having a good year		Reading a newspaper	
Recruiting extra staff			

1.2   Listen again. Complete these sentences about the things that are happening.

1   _____ _____ writing a report.   _____ _____ an article for *Business News*.
2   Our Sales Department _____ _____ a lot of extra staff.
3   _____ _____ some visitors round the building.
4   I'm afraid _____ _____ _____ many orders.
5   I'm _____ _____ it at the moment.

2   Controlled practice

2.1   Read the conversations. Make the correct verb form from the words given in brackets.

1
JOHN: _____ (you/do) anything at the moment?
TIM: Nothing special. _____ (I/wait) for a telephone call.
JOHN: _____ (I/not/do) anything either. Let's have some coffee.

2
SUE: Where's Clive?
ANN: _____ (He/give) a talk at the sales conference.
SUE: _____ (he/talk) about the new XR300 model?
ANN: No, _____ (he/not/deal) with it today. _____ (He/explain) our
        new advertising campaign.

3
JANE: _____ (My feet/kill) me! I must sit down. _____ (anyone/sit) in
        this chair?
ALEX: No. Helen was here, but _____ (she/use) the photocopier at the
        moment.

4
MR CHOI: How _____ (the company/get on)?
MR SAKO: _____ (It/do) very well. _____ (We/make) good profits,
           and _____ (we/develop) new products.

5   (*This conversation is on the tape.*)
CALLER: Hello, can I speak to Mr Edmonds please?
PA: I'm afraid he isn't available. _____ (He/have) lunch at the moment.
CALLER: Well, this is John Rae speaking. _____ (I/phone) from our Italian
          office. _____ (I/visit) our suppliers here. Can you ask Mr Edmonds
          to call me back?

2.2   Make sentences about the following people in Bentel. Use the simple present and present continuous forms, as in the example.

1   Mr Wang: Finance Department/record payments/have lunch.
Mr Wang works in the Finance Department. Usually, he records payments. But he isn't recording payments at the moment. He's having lunch.

2   Miss Farid: Personnel Department/deal with staff problems/meet some new trainees.

3   Mrs Bianco: Sales Department/sell goods to customers/fill in an expense claim.

4   John and Frank: Production Department/maintain the machines/play golf.

5   Harry and Jack: Warehouse/load goods onto trucks/take goods to a customer.

6   I: Promotions Department/send out catalogues/design a poster.

3   Activity

3.1   *Description.* Look at the times on the chart. Tell your partner about things that you think are happening NOW in your company and in companies around the world. For example:

Most of the employees are working.
The secretaries are typing letters.
The managers are having meetings.
The factory is manufacturing goods ..., etc.

To practise negative sentences, also say things that are NOT happening (e.g. if it is night and nobody is at work). For example:

> Most of the employees aren't working at the moment. They're watching TV at home.
> The secretaries aren't typing letters. They're attending evening classes.
> etc.

3.2   *Making excuses for another person.* Look again at Conversation 5 in Exercise 2.1. (Note: You can hear this conversation on the tape.) Have similar conversations with a partner. Follow this plan:

> CALLER: Hello, can I speak to ... please?
> PA: I'm afraid he/she isn't available. He's/She's ... at the moment.
> CALLER: Well, this is ... speaking. I'm phoning from ...
> (*finish the conversation any way you like*)

3.3   *Invitations and refusals.* Give invitations to other students and refuse them, as in the example below. (Note: You can hear this example on the tape.) Use your own ideas for the phrases in brackets.

> A: Would you like to ... (come and have a drink)?
> B: I'm afraid I can't. I'm ... (writing a report) at the moment.

4   Language reference

To talk about the situation NOW we usually use the present continuous tense. This has *am, are, is* and a verb ending in *-ing*:

Questions

Are you Is she	writing	a report?

Positive statements

I'm You're She's	writing	a report.

I'm = I am
You're = You are
She's = She is

Negative statements

I'm not	writing	a report.
You aren't		
She isn't		

I'm = I am not
You aren't = You are not
She isn't = She is not

Notes:
1 In everyday speech (but not formal writing) we use 'short' forms. For example, we say *she's writing* instead of *she **is** writing, we **aren't** writing* instead of *we **are not** writing*.
2 We do not use the short forms so often with subjects which are not pronouns, e.g. *Mary, our company, the Managing Director.*
3 Notice that we say *I'm not* NOT 'I amn't'.
4 The present continuous has a different meaning from the simple present:
    Mary *writes* reports every day. (simple present for regular actions)
    Mary *is writing* a report now. (present continuous for actions NOW).

Inviting and refusing

Would you like to (come and have a drink)?
I'm afraid I can't. I'm (writing a report) at the moment.

Asking for a person by telephone; excusing

Can I speak to (Mr Smith), please?
I'm afraid he isn't available.
He's (having lunch) at the moment.

Places (1): Saying where people and things are

(prepositions; location phrases; specifying objects by their location)

1 Listening focus

1.1 *Basic locations with 'at' and 'in'.* Listen. Choose *at* or *in* in the sentences next to the pictures. Write in these names (the first is done for you).

Miss Connor	Mr Long	Mr Renaldo
Mrs Pereira	Mr Cox	Mr Fisher

Miss Connor is at/(in) a showroom.

_____ is at/in a meeting.

_____ is at/in a reception desk.

36

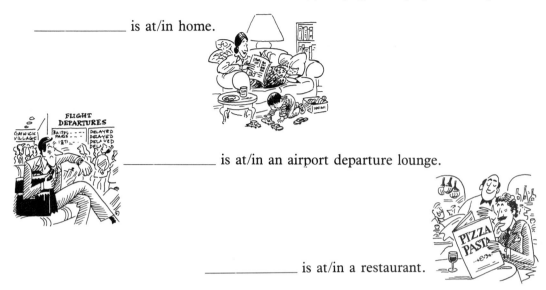

_____ is at/in home.

_____ is at/in an airport departure lounge.

_____ is at/in a restaurant.

1.2 *Mixed location phrases*. Listen. Look at the picture. Write down the names of things in the picture and where they are. The first is done for you.

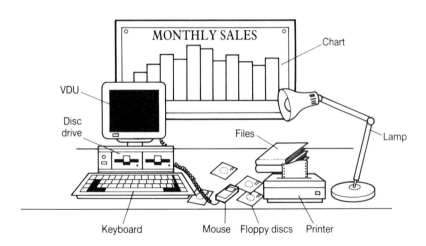

1 *computer*   (_____*on*_____ the desk)
2 _____ (_____ the disc drive)
3 _____ (_____ the desk, _____ the lamp)
4 _____ (_____ the disc drive)
5 _____ (_____ the keyboard and the printer)
6 _____ (_____ the floppy discs)
7 _____ (_____ the wall, _____ the desk)
8 _____ (_____ the chart)
9 _____ (_____ the printer)

2   Controlled practice

2.1   *'At' or 'in'.* Read these instructions to a service engineer. Complete the sentences with *at* or *in*.

1   Please make a service call to Mr Harris, living _____ 2, Harbour Street. His VCR is out of order.
2   He lives _____ an apartment, _____ the top of a modern building.
3   It's the highest building _____ the city, so it's easy to find.
4   On the way there, call _____ our branch _____ Hill Street.
5   You'll find Mr Wong _____ the service desk. He has spare parts for most VCRs.
6   Write the details of any repairs _____ the repairs book.
7   But remember that we do all major repairs _____ our main workshop.
8   So don't waste too much time trying to repair the VCR _____ the house.
9   Just put it _____ the van and bring it back here.

2.2   *Specifying items and their locations.* Look at the drawings. Complete the conversations. Choose phrases from this list (use them more than once if necessary).

Where is it?	The one on the left	above the filing cabinet
Which one?	The one on the right	next to the calendar
it's over there	The one in the middle of	in front of the window
it's among	The one at the top of	behind the screen

1   ALEC: Can you bring me the file
on Bentel, please?
   BILL: _____ ? There's
a pile of them here.
   ALEC: _____ the pile.

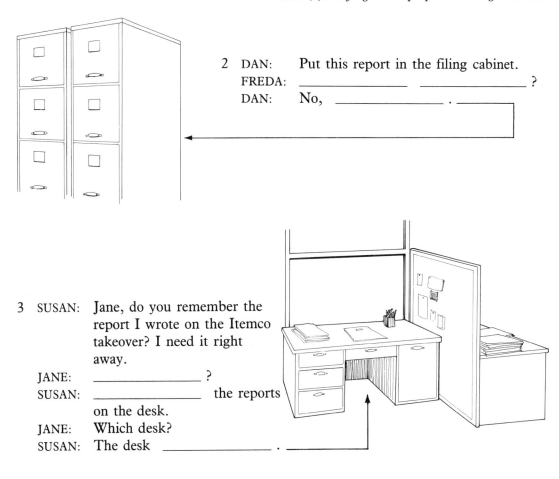

2 DAN: Put this report in the filing cabinet.
  FREDA: _____ _____ ?
  DAN: No, _____ . _____

3 SUSAN: Jane, do you remember the
          report I wrote on the Itemco
          takeover? I need it right
          away.
  JANE: _____ ?
  SUSAN: _____ the reports
          on the desk.
  JANE: Which desk?
  SUSAN: The desk _____ . _____

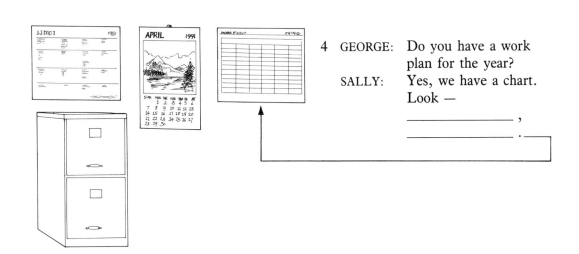

4 GEORGE: Do you have a work
           plan for the year?
  SALLY: Yes, we have a chart.
           Look —

           _____ ,
           _____ . _____

3 Activity

3.1   Describe the layout of objects in an office or room in your place of work. Your partner tries to draw a rough plan from your description.

3.2   Arrange to meet your partner after work. Use phrases like those below.

S1:   Where can we meet?
S2:   Let's meet ...
         ... at the front gate, at the entrance, at the bus stop.
         ... in the bar, in the foyer, in the car park.
S1:   That isn't very suitable for me. Let's meet at/in ...
         (and so on)

3.3   Give instructions connected with things in your classroom, company or town. Do not be exact at first. Ask and answer (specifying locations) until the answer is clear. For example:

S1:   Put this sheet of paper in the folder.
S2:   Which folder?
S1:   The one on the table.
S2:   Which table?
S1:   The table in front of the window.
S2:   OK.

4 Language reference

At versus *in*

- Use *at* when you think of a place as a point, NOT something that goes round you.

- Use *in* when you think of something that goes round you, like a room, or water, or a city.

- Use *at* to talk about:
         Buildings used for their normal purpose:
            Mr Braun is *at* the warehouse. (= the place where he usually works).
         Towns on the way to a place
            We stop *at* Beijing on the way to Tokyo.
         Addresses:
            I live *at* 14, Independence Street.
         Specific places, that don't go round you:
            I'll see you *at* the gate.

Note also:

> *at* home, *at* work, *at* the top/bottom, *at* the front/back (of a building)

- Use *in* to talk about:

  Buildings, when we think of the actual building and its parts:
  > There's a payphone *in* the main block.
  > Mary is *in* the canteen at the moment.

  Most towns and countries:
  > Mr de Silva lives *in* Madrid, which is *in* Spain.

  Streets, rows, lines, queues:
  > I live *in* Independence Street.
  > Let's take a seat *in* the front row.

Specifying location

These words and phrases are common when talking about things in an office, classroom, building, etc.:

above (something)	on the left/right (of something)
among (several things)	at the top/bottom (of something)
behind (something)	in the middle (of something)
beside (something)	
between (one thing and another)	It's over there (pointing to something)
in front of (something)	
near (something)	
next to (= beside and very near something)	
under (something)	

Specifying objects by their location

A: Can you bring me the OBJECT, please?
B: Which one?
A: The one ... (IN A PARTICULAR PLACE).

Places (2): Directions

(direction phrases; prepositions; question forms; ordinal numbers)

1 Listening focus

1.1   Look at the plan opposite of the headquarters of Exton Books. Listen to the places asked for. (The visitors are all talking to the receptionist.) Write the numbers 1–5 in the plan, beside the places asked for. Number 1 is marked as an example.

1.2   Listen again. Fill in the sentences.

1 VISITOR: Excuse me. _____ for the Sales Department.
   R'TIONIST: _____ ? It's _____ , on _____ .

2 VISITOR: Er ... Could you _____ me _____ to
               the Managing Director's office?
   R'TIONIST: Yes. _____ to _____ . It's the
               _____ on the _____ as you
               _____ the lift.

3 VISITOR: _____ me. _____ the showroom?
   R'TIONIST: It's on _____ , through _____ there.

4 VISITOR: _____ me _____ the Art and Design
               department _____ , please?
   R'TIONIST: Yes. _____ to _____ . It's
               _____ the corridor, next to the lift.

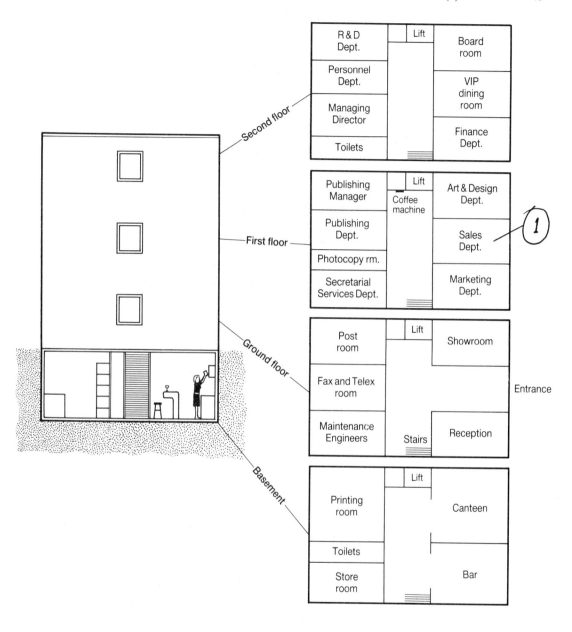

5 R'TIONIST: Can I _____ ?
  VISITOR: Yes, _____ the printing room. _____ to
             service one of the machines.
  R'TIONIST: Just go _____ . It's _____ .

2 Controlled practice

2.1   Write questions and answers, or practise with a partner. Use the plan on page 43.

Questions

Excuse me. I'm looking for		the	Personnel Department	.	
Where's Where are			Publishing Manager fax and telex room toilets	, please?	
Can you tell me	how to get to		Managing Director bar	, please?	
	where		coffee machine photocopy room maintenance engineers	is, are,	please?

Answers

It's They're	upstairs, on the	first second	floor.
It's They're	downstairs, in the basement.		
It's They're	on this floor — that door there.		

2.2   Look again at the plan on page 43. Which person, room or department do these instructions direct you to? Write the answer in the blanks.

1   It's on the ground floor, opposite the entrance.   _____
2   It's on the first floor — the second door on the right as you come from the lift. _____

3   They're on the top floor — the first door on the left as you come from the stairs. _____

4   Go up the stairs to the first floor. He's at the end of the corridor, on the left. _____

5   Take the lift to the second floor. It's the second room on the left as you come from the lift. _____

6   Go downstairs to the basement. It's the first room on the right, at the bottom of the stairs. _____

Now write QUESTIONS to match the answers above. Try to use different ways of forming the questions.

2.3 Here are some questions and answers about places in the Richman School of Business. Write the questions and answers with the words in their correct order.

1 Q: the library? / me. / Where's / Excuse
   A: upstairs, / first / on / It's / the / floor.

2 Q: me. / for / I'm / looking / Excuse / the Director of Studies.
   A: the / door / the / on / right. / fourth / upstairs — / She's

3 Q: please? / you / is, / where / tell / me / Can / the office
   A: that / there. / It's / through / door

4 Q: the coffee bar? / me / to / to / Can / you / tell / how / get
   A: downstairs, / in / basement. / It's / the

5 Q: the Business Administration Department. / looking / I'm / for
   A: stairs. / the / It's / upstairs — /come / from / door / second / the / left / as / you / the / on

6 Q: is, / Can / the Director's private apartment / where / you / tell / please? / me
   A: top / Take / to / the / the / lift / floor.
      at / It's / the / the / corridor. / end / of

3 Activity

3.1 Work with other students like this:

YOU: say how to get to a room or department in your college or place of work. (It must be a place that other students know about.) Do not say the name of the room or department.
OTHER STUDENTS: work out the place you are talking about.

3.2 Practise the roles of visitor and receptionist with a partner. Decide on a suitable building to talk about. Ask for and give directions. (Note: It is best if you talk about buildings which the receptionist knows but the visitor doesn't know well.)

3.3 *Information gap*. Student A looks at the plan below. Student B looks at the plan on page 138.

Student A

Look at the floor plan. It shows the plan of the Bentel Corporation Building. Ask for and give information about how to get to the people and places located in the building.

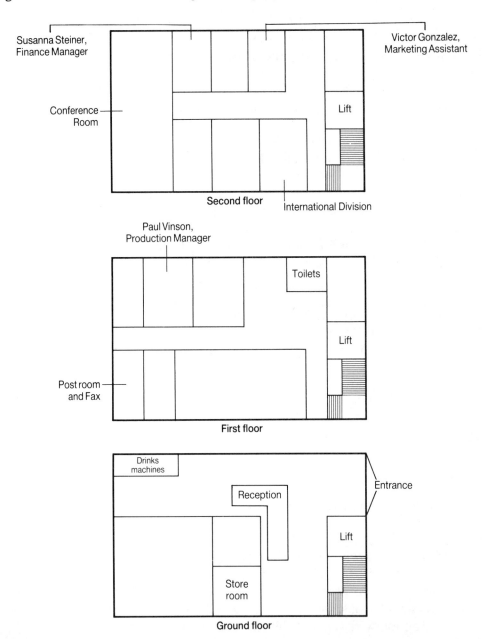

Label your plan.

Ask for:
Robert Khan, the Marketing Manager
Victoria Machin, the Sales Assistant
Ask to make a photocopy
Stuart McFarlane, the Production Assistant
The Director
The Personnel Department
Charles Kettering, the Sales Manager
The Director's secretary

4 Language reference

Asking for directions

Excuse me.
Where's ...?/Where are ...?
I'm looking for ...
Can you tell me where ... is/are, please?
Can you tell me how to get to ..., please?

Giving directions

It's upstairs/downstairs.
      on the first/second/third/fourth/fifth/etc. floor.
      on this floor/on the ground floor.
      in the basement.
      at the end of the corridor.
      through that door there.

Go upstairs to the second floor.
Take the lift (up) to the second floor.

It's the second door on the right as you come from the lift.
It's the third door on the left as you come from the stairs.

Prepositions of movement

to the first floor
from the stairs
from/out of the lift
through the fire doors

Other prepositions commonly used in directions

opposite the canteen
next to the Director's office

Ordinal numbers (for floors, doors, etc.)

the   first   floor   on the right, etc.
      second   door
      third
      fourth
      fifth
      sixth
      seventh
      eighth
      ninth
      tenth
      etc.

Note: In Britain the floor you enter from the street is the *ground* floor (and the next floor up is the first floor). In the USA the floor you enter from the street is the *first* floor.

UNIT 10

Quantity (1): Availability

(*some/any; have got*; office and restaurant inquiries; suggestions; offers)

1   Listening focus

1.1   Listen to three conversations in an office. Mark the items below with a tick (✓) if they ARE in the office, and with a cross (✗) if they are NOT in the office. The first is done for you.

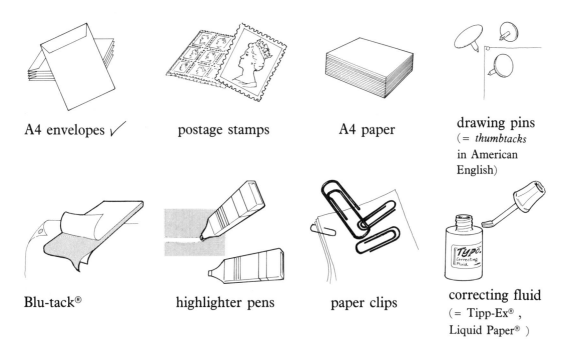

A4 envelopes ✓   postage stamps   A4 paper   drawing pins
(= *thumbtacks*
in American
English)

Blu-tack®   highlighter pens   paper clips   correcting fluid
(= Tipp-Ex®,
Liquid Paper®)

1.2   (a) Listen again to the first conversation. Complete these phrases from it.

A: Are there _____ A4 envelopes?
B: Yes, I've got _____ in this drawer.
A: How about postage stamps? Have you got _____ ?
B: No, I'm afraid there aren't _____ here.
A: By the way, we haven't got _____ A4 paper left.
B: Maybe you can get _____ from the stationery store.

(b) In the phrases above, find an example of the following:

• A person INQUIRES if something is available.
• A person says something IS available.
• A person says something ISN'T available.

(c) Listen again to Conversation 2. What SUGGESTION can you hear in it?
    Listen again to Conversation 3. What OFFER can you hear in it?

2   Controlled practice

2.1   Read these conversations between some business executives in a restaurant, and a waiter. Complete the sentences with *some* or *any*.

1   WAITER: Would you like _____ wine, madam?
    ANNA: Yes, please. Have you got _____ white wine, not too sweet?
    WAITER: I can recommend our house wine. Can I offer you _____ to taste?

2   GEORGE: We'd like _____ mineral water please. Is there _____ Vittel® ?
    WAITER: Ah no, we haven't got _____ Vittel® , but perhaps you would like _____ Perrier® . Shall I bring _____ bottles — two or three perhaps?

3   MIKE: Are there _____ vegetarian dishes? I can't see _____ on the menu.
    WAITER: We have _____ excellent egg dishes. You'll find _____ here on the à la carte menu.
    MIKE: Ah yes. And I see you have _____ salads as well. An omelette with a green salad, please.

4   GEORGE: How about _____ cheese? Shall we have _____ ?
    ANNA: I don't want _____ , but the rest of you can have _____ if you want.
    WAITER: I'll bring _____ different kinds of cheese and you can help yourselves.

2.2   In the conversations above, find an example of:

- An inquiry about availability
- A positive answer
- A negative answer
- An offer
- A suggestion

3   Activity

3.1   *Information gap.*

Student B
Turn to page 140.

Student A
Look at this check-list. It shows some of the things that are or aren't in your office. You have some of the information. Your partner has the rest.

Blu-tack®	☐	erasers	X	scotch tape	✓
correcting fluid	☐	felt-tip pens	X	staples	☐
drawing pins	✓	glue	X	stamps	☐
envelopes	☐	paper clips	☐	typing paper	✓

Ask and answer questions like this, and fill in the check-list.

    Q: Have we got any ... (glue, etc.)
    A: Yes, we've got some. We don't need any.
         or   No, we haven't got any. We need some.

3.2   Work with a partner. Imagine that you have invited your partner (e.g. a business colleague, your boss) for a meal. OFFER things to eat and drink. Your partner accepts or refuses. For example:

YOU: Would you like some ... (wine, vegetables, salad, meat, cheese, etc.)?
YOUR PARTNER: Yes, please. {That would be lovely.
                              {It looks very nice, etc.
        or   No thanks. {I can't eat any more.
                         {I never eat cheese/I never drink wine ... etc.

Now YOU and YOUR PARTNER switch the parts round.

3.3 Work with two or three other students. This time, imagine you are making SUGGESTIONS about things to eat in a restaurant. For example:

YOU: Shall we have some ... (cheese, wine, etc.)?
  or How about some ... (cheese, wine, etc.)?
ANOTHER STUDENT: That sounds nice. I'd like some.
                  or I don't want any. But the rest of you can have some.
                  or I'd rather have some ... (fruit, etc.)

Now other students in the group make suggestions. At the end, one of you gives an order to the 'waiter'.

4   Language reference

Some and *any*

Some and *any* are used to talk about INDEFINITE quantities (= quantities we do not know exactly). They are used with UNCOUNTABLE words (like *water, paper, efficiency*) and with PLURAL words (like *letters, employees, computers*).

Some is used:
• In positive statements:
    I've got *some* typing paper here.
    There are *some* stamps in the drawer.
• In suggestions:
    How about *some* cheese?
• In offers:
    Would you like *some* wine?

Any is used:
• In negative statements:
    We haven't got *any* A4 paper here.
    There aren't *any* paper clips in this drawer.
• In most questions:
    Is there *any* typing paper?
    Have we got *any* postage stamps?

Forms of *have got*

Positive statements

I've/we've/you've/they've	got	some letters to write.
He's/She's		

Negative statements

I/we/you/they haven't	got	any envelopes.
He/She hasn't		

Questions

Have I/we/you/they	got	any appointments today?
Has he/she		

Use of *have got* and *have* on its own

There is not much difference between *have got* and *have* on its own when we talk about things that are available, and things that belong to us. Usually both forms are correct. There are some small differences:

- *Have* on its own is used more for PERMANENT things. *Have got* is used more for TEMPORARY things (things that come and go):
  We have a large permanent staff.
  We've got some temps (= temporary secretaries) working here just now.

- *Have* on its own is sometimes more FORMAL than *have got*. Compare:
  1 WAITER: *We have* some excellent egg dishes.
  2 WAITER: *We've got* some nice egg dishes.
  Sentence 1 gives the idea of a high-class, expensive restaurant.
  Sentence 2 suggests an informal, relaxed atmosphere.

Ways of making suggestions

How about ... (some cheese, etc.)?
Shall we ... (have some cheese, etc.)?

Ways of offering something

Would you like ... (some wine, etc.)?
Shall I ... (bring some wine, etc.)?
Can I offer you ... (some wine, etc.)? (rather formal)

UNIT 11

Reporting actions and events

(reporting using the simple past tense)

54

UNIT 11

Reporting actions and events

(reporting using the simple past tense)

1 Listening focus

1.1 Listen to the conversations. Which of the following statements are TRUE and which are FALSE, according to the conversations? The first is done for you.

1 I sent the invoice last week.	*FALSE*
2 IBC didn't sign the contract for computer hardware.	
3 You stayed at the Intercontinental Hotel.	
4 Stephen bought the equipment.	
5 We didn't supply all the goods they wanted.	
6 Our agents sold the goods at too high a price.	
7 I found San Bernardo a very interesting place.	
8 I felt angry about the meeting this morning.	
9 I didn't write down all the details of the proposal.	
10 My company showed their newest model, the C-300.	

1.2 Listen again. Write the verb phrases in the table below, as in the examples given. ALL the phrases are in the conversations.

	Question	Negative statements	Positive statements
1	*Did you send?*	*I didn't send*	*I sent*
2	*Did IBC sign?*	*They didn't sign*	*They signed*
3	*Did I stay?*		
4			
5			
6			
7			
8			
9			
10			

Which verbs are REGULAR (positive form ends in -*ed*)? Which are IRREGULAR?

2 **Controlled practice**

2.1   *Reporting after a trip.* Read the conversation. Below, write the correct form of the verbs in italics. Some of the verbs become QUESTIONS, some become NEGATIVE forms, and some DO NOT CHANGE. If there is no change, put a dash (—). The first is done for you.

JOE: How ¹*your trip went?*
TIM: ²*It went* very well. ³*I visited* the Fabiani factory in Milan.
JOE: What ⁴*you thought* of it?
TIM: ⁵*It looked* very impressive. ⁶*I spoke* to the Manager, Signor Verdi. ⁷*He seemed* very interested in doing business with us.
JOE: ⁸*You discussed* our plan for having a European partner?
TIM: Yes, ⁹*I told* him about it. ¹⁰*He asked* me to arrange a meeting with you. However, ¹¹*I made* any definite arrangement.
JOE: I'll phone him. ¹²*You met* the Director of ETL?
TIM: No, ¹³*I managed* to meet him. He was away. But ¹⁴*I met* his assistant. ¹⁵*We had* an interesting conversation.
JOE: Good. And when ¹⁶*you got* back?
TIM: Last night. In fact ¹⁷*the plane arrived* after midnight.
JOE: You must be tired. Take things easy today.

1 *did your trip go* _____   10 _____
2 _____   11 _____
3 _____   12 _____
4 _____   13 _____
5 _____   14 _____
6 _____   15 _____
7 _____   16 _____
8 _____   17 _____
9 _____

2.2   *Forming questions.* Read the sentences below. They were said by an employee returning from a trip.

1 I found out *some interesting information.*
2 The Manager took me to *the warehouse.*
3 He showed me *their stock control system.*
4 They installed it in *1989.*
5 They chose *the XL-200* system.
6 It performed *magnificently.*
7 The computer engineers gave *excellent* service.
8 They connected the regional branches to the system *last May.*
9 The Manager recommended *a similar system.*

Imagine that the room is noisy and you do not hear the words in italics. What questions can you ask? Complete the questions below. The first is done for you.

1 What _did you find out ?_
2 Where _____ you?
3 What _____ you?
4 When _____ it?
5 What system _____ ?
6 How _____ ?
7 What kind of service _____ ?
8 When _____ the regional branches?
9 What _____ ?

3 Activity

3.1 Work with a partner like this:

Student A
Report to your partner about things you did yesterday, or earlier today. Think of answers to these questions:
  What did you do?
  When did you do it?
  Who did you meet?
  Where did you go?

Student B
Listen, but ask your partner questions while you listen, to make sure that you understand the facts. For example:
  How long did you stay there?
  Why did you do that?
  What did you think of . . . (a person, place)?

3.2 Work with a partner as in 3.1 above, but this time imagine that you have just come back from a business trip. Tell your partner about the factories you visited, the people you met, the deals you made . . . and so on. Include some great successes and some terrible failures!

Your partner asks you questions and takes notes. Later he/she can try to summarise your report to the rest of the class.

3.3 Have a race with your partner. See who is first to find the irregular past forms and the verbs they come from, rearranging the jumbled letters. The first is done for you.

	Irregular past form		Verb which it comes from	
1	AWS	*SAW*	EES	*SEE*
2	WELF		LYF	
3	UGHTAT		CHEAT	
4	SLOD		LESL	
5	OUGHTB		YUB	
6	ENTS		ENDS	
7	EMANT		AMEN	
8	GENAB		GNIBE	
9	VEROD		DIVER	
10	AIPD		YAP	
11	OLTS		EOLS	
12	DARE		ARED	
13	WERG		RGWO	
14	TEROW		WTREI	
15	GHTUHOT		TNIKH	
16	DAME		EMAK	
17	EAMC		CEMO	
18	SEKOP		EAKPS	
19	SORE		IRES	
20	ABET		TEAB	

4 Language reference

Uses and forms of the simple past

We use the simple past tense to talk about actions at a definite time in the past. Sometimes we mention the time:

John arrived *yesterday*.

If the time is understood, we don't need to mention it:

We *enjoyed* ourselves. We *stayed* in a nice hotel and *saw* some interesting places. (in answer to a question about a recent holiday)

The simple past is easy because the ending does not change for *I*, *you*, *he*, etc. We say:

I *walked*, you *walked*, he *walked*, and so on.

REGULAR verbs have the ending *-ed* in the positive form:

I ask*ed* (from *ask*)   I stop*ped* (from *stop*)
I smil*ed* (from *smile*)   I tri*ed* (from *try*)

IRREGULAR verbs have many different endings. For example:

I *began* (from *begin*)   I *went* (from *go*)
I *found* (from *find*)   I *came* (from *come*)

Questions have *did*, like this:

Did you ask?
Did he begin?
Did they go?

Negative sentences have *didn't* (= *did not* in writing), like this:

You *didn't* ask
He *didn't* begin
They *didn't* go

Was and *were* (= past forms of *be*)

Positive statements

I/he/she/it We/you/they	was were	in the office.

Questions

Was Were	I/he/she/it we/you/they	in the office?

Negative statements

I/he/she/it We/you/they	wasn't weren't	in the office.

wasn't = was not
weren't = were not

Remember also *there was* and *there were*:

There was a representative from Nafco at the conference.
There were some interesting new models at the exhibition.

Quantity (2): Large and small quantities

(a lot (of), (not) much/many, a few/a little, very few/very little)

1 Listening focus

1.1 Listen. Tick the items according to what you hear. The first is done for you.

Item	a **LARGE** quantity	a **SMALL** quantity
1 Employees		✓
2 Discussion		
3 Information		
4 Overseas customers		
5 Books		
6 Subcontractors		
7 Training		
8 Help from others		

1.2   Listen again. Can you pick out the actual 'quantity' phrases? The first is done for you.

1   Employees;   just ____*a*____ ____*few*____
2   Discussion: _____ _____ of discussion
3   Information: a _____, but not _____
4   Overseas customers: not _____
5   Books: very _____
6   Subcontractors: just _____ _____
7   Training: _____ _____ of training
8   Help from others: very _____ help

2   Controlled practice

2.1   Choose the correct form in these sentences.

1   A: How *much/many* time have we got?
    B: We've *a little/a few* time before the next meeting.

2   A: Were there *much/many* people at the trade exhibition?
    B: There were *a few/a little*, but not *many/much* from our company.

3   A: I've got *a lot of/a lot* ideas for new products.
    B: Good. We haven't had *much/many* success with our products recently.

4   A: Does your company have *much/many* sales representatives in Germany?
    B: Yes, quite *a lot of/a lot*. In fact we have over a hundred.

5 A: How *much/many* advice did you get before you started the job?
   B: Oh, *very little/a little* I didn't ask for other people's ideas.

6 A: I suppose *a lot of/much* people telephoned during my absence.
   B: Actually, there were *very little/very few* telephone calls — everyone is on holiday at the moment.

2.2 Complete the sentences with these words and phrases:

a lot   much   a few   very few
a lot of   many   a little   very little

1 How _____ kilometres did you travel, and how _____ petrol did you use?

2 Our Promotions Department put out _____ publicity about our new products. As a result, we had quite _____ inquiries.

3 'Did you send out _____ catalogues?'
   'Oh yes, we sent out _____ catalogues — several thousand in fact.'

4 There wasn't _____ advance warning about the accountancy examination, so _____ students got good marks.

5 There were _____ problems when we changed the invoice system, but not _____

6 Galaxy Engineering isn't a well known company; in fact, we have _____ information about it.

7 'Did you have any trouble with this computer?'
   'Just _____ , to start with. The engineers soon put it right.'

8 Tom mentioned _____ interesting new developments in his speech. I was surprised that there weren't _____ questions at the end.

9 We haven't got _____ A4 paper left. When you go to the stationery store, please get _____ . Then we'll have enough for several weeks.

10 I was very interested in their methods. I asked _____ questions, but I didn't get _____ information.

3 Activity

3.1 Look at this list of words. They can all be used in business situations.

equipment	industrial robots
new products	evidence
stationery	software
fuel	money
technicians	credit
job applicants	time
information	sales representatives
competition	expertise
orders	catalogues
brochures	spare capacity

(a) Make sure you know what the words mean. (You can use a dictionary to help you with this.)

(b) Think of situations in which you could use the words.

(c) Decide whether the words are PLURAL or UNCOUNTABLE (i.e. which question do we use with them — *How many?* or *How much?*).

3.2 *Information gap*. Student B turns to page 140. Student A reads the instructions below.

Student A
Ask Student B questions about the items listed in 3.1. The questions:
• should be connected with a company (real or imaginary).
• should have some details to make them sound 'real'.
• should begin with *How much . . .?* or *How many . . .?* For example:

How many brochures did we print for our new advertising campaign?
How many catalogues did we send to our customers?
How much competition do we expect?
How many job applicants . . .?
(and so on)

Student B will answer according to the information he/she has.

4   Language reference

Quantity expressions with plurals and uncountables

For a large quantity we can say *a lot* and *a lot of*:
Are there any orders for the new machine?
Oh yes, *a lot*. There are *a lot of* orders.
Is there any interest in the new machine?
Oh yes, *a lot*. There's *a lot of* interest.

Note: *A lot of* comes before a noun, but *a lot* stands on its own.

For slightly smaller quantities we often use *QUITE a lot (of)*:
quite a lot of people, *quite a lot of* interest.

For quantities in the middle of the scale and indefinite quantities we can use *some*:
At the meeting there were *some* representatives from our German branch.

For small quantities we use *a few* (with PLURAL words only) or *a little* (with UNCOUNTABLE words only):
We have only *a few* orders for the new machine.
There was only *a little* interest in the new machine.

To talk about quantities in a negative way we can use *not many* (with PLURAL words) and *not much* (with UNCOUNTABLE words):
I'm afraid there are*n't many* orders.
I'm afraid there was*n't much* interest.

To talk about very small quantities we can use *very few* (with PLURALS) and *very little* (with UNCOUNTABLES). These expressions also give a negative idea.
There were *very few* representatives from our German branch.
There was *very little* interest in the new machine.

We use *much* and *many* in questions:
How *many* orders did we get? Did we get *many* orders?
How *much* interest was there? Was there *much* interest?

Quantity expression on a scale

A LARGE QUANTITY

NONE

a lot, a lot of
quite a lot, quite a lot of
some (= an indefinite quantity)
a few, a little
not many, not much
very few, very little ──── (negative idea)

UNIT 13

The situation up to now

(present perfect tense for past leading up to present)

EARLIER.....   NOW

1 Listening focus

1.1 Listen to the conversations on the tape. A sentence is missing at the end of each conversation.

Now listen again. Match the conversations on the tape with the sentences (a)–(h) that come at the end. The first is done for you.

Conversation 1 __*e*__   (a) But I believe they're very reliable.
Conversation 2 _____   (b) There's her briefcase on the desk.
Conversation 3 _____   (c) I like it here.
Conversation 4 _____   (d) He has a lot of friends in the government.
Conversation 5 _____   (e) They're ready to post now.
Conversation 6 _____   (f) He's still in Japan.
Conversation 7 _____   (g) But it refuses to accept a shorter working week.
Conversation 8 _____   (h) The news is really astonishing!

1.2   Listen to the conversation again. This time WRITE OUT sentences from the tape ALONG WITH the sentences (a)–(h) that come after them, as in these examples:

Sentence on the tape	**Sentence after it**
1 Yes, I've typed all the letters.	They're ready to post now.
2 No, he hasn't come back yet.	He's still in Japan.
(and so on)	

What do the sentences on the right describe — something in the past or something NOW?

2   Controlled practice

Complete the conversations. Use the present perfect with a suitable form of the words in brackets.

1 (*before a meeting*)
TOM: Where's David? _____ (anyone/see) him?
ANN: I don't know. I _____ (not/see) him this morning.
JOE: I _____ (just/spoke) to him. He's on his way here now.

2 (*at a training session*)
INSTRUCTOR: Listen everyone — _____ (you/do) Unit 24?
STUDENT 1:   No. We _____ (not/get) to Unit 24 yet.
STUDENT 2:   Yes we have. We _____ (finish) Unit 24. We
_____ (start) Unit 25 now.

3 (*talking about the company*)
ALEC: There _____ (be) a lot of changes in our department this year.
BOB: Yes. The new manager _____ (change) everything.
ALEC: _____ (he/reorganise) your department as well?
BOB: Yes. And a lot of people _____ (leave) because they weren't happy about the changes.

4 (*in an office*)
MARY: _____ (you/take) the envelopes out of this drawer?
SUE: I _____ (not/touch) the envelopes. I _____ (not/send) any letters today.
MARY: Well, _____ (someone/take) them. There was a packet of envelopes here this morning.
SUE: Ask Helen. _____ (she/have) so many letters to type recently. Perhaps _____ (she/take) them.

3 Activity

3.1 Work with other students. Think of sentences which could go in the blanks below, leading up to the sentences which are given. The sentences should contain a present perfect form (*have/has* + past participle). Use a negative form when you see *not* in brackets.

1 _____. We expect our sales to improve dramatically next year.

2 _____. In our view, the company's offer is totally unacceptable.

3 _____. It has debts of more than 20 million US dollars.

4 (*not*) _____. We are still waiting for some of the staff to arrive.

5 (*not*) _____. Perhaps it's because he has a lot of family problems.

6 _____. He's doing a very good job now.

7 _____. If you need evidence, look at these figures.

8 (*not*) _____. Perhaps they're on strike.

9 (*not*) _____. Her coat and handbag are still here.

10 _____. Together, the two companies now form the biggest electronics group in the country.

3.2 Go round the class. Find students who have done various things TODAY by asking questions like this:

Have you said 'Good morning' to your boss/your friends/the secretary?
Have you shown your boss that you are keen and efficient?
Have you read the financial pages of the newspaper?
Have you read the sports/gossip/fashion pages of the newspaper?
Have you made any telephone calls?
Have you bought anything?
Have you made any business deals?
Have you travelled in a bus/a taxi?
etc.

Take a note of any positive answers you get. Later you can report them, for example:

(Tomiko) has said 'Good morning' to (her) boss.

3.3   Work with a group of students. Think of interesting or amusing questions you can ask with *ever*. For example:

> Have you ever told a lie in an expense claim?
> Have you ever travelled first class in an aeroplane?

Now go round the students in other groups and obtain answers. Later you can report answers like this:

> (Fifteen) students say they have never told a lie in an expense claim.
> (Two) students say they have travelled first class in an aeroplane.

4   Language reference

Use of present perfect

To show a connection between the past and the situation NOW, we use the present perfect:
> John *has arrived*. (= He is here NOW)

We can use the present perfect:
- When we started doing something in the past and are STILL doing it:
  > *I've worked* for this company for thirty years (and I STILL work for them).

- When we did something in the past that has RESULTS now:
  > I've worked hard all my life (and as a RESULT I am rich now).

- When we talk about things at NO SPECIFIC TIME in the past, things that are still part of our lives:
  > *I've worked* for a lot of different companies. (NO SPECIFIC TIME mentioned)

The present perfect often occurs with *ever, never, just*:
> Have you *ever* been to Italy?
> No, I've *never* been there.
> I've *just* come back from Italy.

Form of present perfect

The present perfect contains *have* or *has* and the past participle. REGULAR past participles end in *-ed* (e.g. I've ask*ed*). IRREGULAR past participles end in different ways.

Positive statements
    I've asked (*I've = I have*)
    He's asked (*He's = He has*)
    Tom has asked

Negative statements
    I haven't asked
    He hasn't asked
    Tom hasn't asked

Questions
    Have you asked?
    Has he asked?
    Has Tom asked?

Notes:
1 In formal speech and writing we use *have* and *has*, NOT *'ve* and *'s*.
2 Similarly, with non-pronoun subjects (e.g. *Tom, the company, my friends*) we use *have* and *has*.
3 Notice the forms *there has been* and *there have been*:
    There has been a fire at Bentel.
    There have been problems at the Bentel factory.

Comparison (1): Comparing quantities

(*more, less, fewer;* with the modifers *far* and *slightly*)

1   Listening focus

1.1   Listen to the conversations. Mark these items with a PLUS (+) if the speaker talks about a LARGER amount or number, and a MINUS (–) if the speaker talks about a SMALLER amount or number. The first is done for you.

Orders	+	Power		
Workers		Strikes		
Petrol		Publicity		

1.2   Listen again. Complete the conversations. Each blank stands for one word.

1   A: Have you got many orders this year?
   B: _____ _____ than last year.

2   A: How efficient is your new production system?
   B: Very efficient. We produce the same goods, but with _____ _____ workers.

3   A: What do you think of the new company cars?
   B: They're very economical. They use _____ _____ petrol than the old models.

4   A: I hear that the company is being reorganised.
   B: Yes. It will give the Department Managers _____ _____ power.

5 A: Have there been many strikes this year?

B: _____ _____ than last year.

6 A: Are you happy with the new publicity campaign?

B: Yes. Our products are getting _____ _____ publicity now.

2 Controlled practice

2.1 Make sentences with the same meaning as these sentences. The first is done for you.

1 Axon has slightly more employees than Bentel.

Bentel has slightly fewer employees than Axon.

2 Tom has far more customers than Harry.

Harry _____ .

3 My company has slightly fewer trainees than yours.

Your company _____ .

4 The secretaries here do far more work than the boss.

The boss _____ .

5 I get far less satisfaction from administration than from research.

I _____ .

6 Jan's section has far fewer problems than John's section.

John's section _____ .

7 The Sales Department has slightly more computers than the Production Department.

The Production Department _____ .

2.2   Look at this table of some goods produced by two countries, Eastland and Westland (average production for the last five years).

	Eastland	Westland
Cars	210 000	205 000
Oil	10.2 million barrels	10 million barrels
Computers	100 000	650 000
Steel	500 000 tonnes	1.5 million tonnes
Microwave ovens	33 000	34 000
Rubber	16 000 tonnes	14 500 tonnes
Gold	250 tonnes	3300 tonnes

Now make eight sentences about the two countries from the table below. For example:

Eastland produces slightly more cars than Westland.

Eastland Westland	produces	far slightly	more less fewer	cars oil etc.	than	Westland Eastland

3   Activity

Information gap. Student B turns to page 142. Student A reads these instructions.

Student A
Look at this diagram. It shows how the export of cars by Northland changed between 1980 and 1987. Tell your partner about the diagram. Make sentences like this:
   In 1981, Northland exported slightly more cars than in 1980.

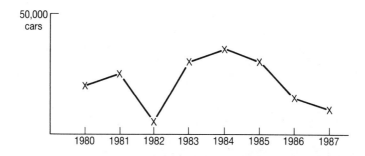

Now listen to your partner's information. Make a rough diagram from the information you hear about exports of oil by Southland, 1980–1987. The start of the diagram is given.

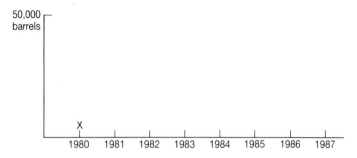

When you have finished, you and your partner check the diagrams you have drawn.

4 Language reference

Comparative forms of quantity words

The words used to compare amounts and numbers are *more, less, fewer*.

To show a greater amount or number we use *more*. It doesn't matter whether the noun is uncountable or plural.

> I need *more* time.   (*time* is uncountable)
> We must sell *more* cars.   (*cars* is plural)

To show a smaller amount we use *less*. The noun must be UNCOUNTABLE.

> Try to use *less* electricity.   (*electricity* is uncountable)

To show a smaller number we use *fewer*. The noun must be PLURAL.

> We have *fewer* employees now.   (*employees* is plural)

Modifying comparisons with *far* and *slightly*

To show bigger and smaller differences we can use *far* and *slightly*, like this:

far	more	power, orders, etc.
slightly	less	power, time, etc.
	fewer	orders, workers, etc.

Comparison (2): Comparing qualities

(comparatives of 'short' and 'long' adjectives; modifying phrases)

1 Listening focus

1.1 Listen to the conversations (you can stop the tape after each conversation). Some words are missing. Complete the conversations with comparative forms of the adjectives below. The first two are done for you.

efficient	successful
big	small
noisy	difficult
short	up-to-date
expensive	cold

Conversation	1	*bigger*
Conversation	2	*more efficient*
Conversation	3	
Conversation	4	
Conversation	5	
Conversation	6	
Conversation	7	
Conversation	8	
Conversation	9	
Conversation	10	

1.2   Now listen to the sentences with the complete comparative forms in them. Check your answers to 1.1.

What kind of words make comparisons with *-er* (e.g. bigg*er*)?
What kind of words make comparisons with *more* (e.g. *more* efficient)?

2   Controlled practice

2.1   Underline the adjectives in the phrases below (e.g. *durable*). (Check that you know the meanings of the adjectives as they are used in the phrases.) Then write a comparative form for each phrase below. (Some phrases have 'long' and some have 'short' adjectives.) The first is done for you.

1   a durable product   *a more durable product*
2   enthusiastic management
3   innovative methods
4   tough bargaining
5   a happy workforce
6   an impressive performance
7   a cheap model
8   economical fuel consumption
9   an unpredictable situation
10   fierce competition
11   high interest rates
12   healthy profits

2.2   *Spelling of 'short' comparatives.*   Choose the correct form.

1   If the weather gets much *hotter/hoter* we'll have to close the factory.
2   Today the pound is slightly *weakker/weaker* against the dollar.

3 Our cleaning service will make your offices a lot *cleanner/cleaner*.
4 It is becoming quite a lot *easyer/easier* to export goods to Japan.
5 We are replacing our *oldr/older* models.
6 Our new models have a much *thickker/thicker* layer of insulation.
7 We are going to make our accounting procedures much *simpleer/simpler*.
8 John feels a lot *happer/happier* in his new job.

2.3 *'Short' comparative forms and modifying phrases.*

(a) Complete the sentences using a comparative form of these adjectives:

low, bad, noisy, heavy, fair, light, large, hot, nice, good, busy

1 Our new model is popular because it only weighs 7 kilos. At 8.5 kilos, our old model
   was _____ .

2 We've re-designed our products. The colours were a little too dark. Now they're
   _____ .

3 (*before a trip*) The weather in Tropicalia is comfortable at the moment, but it will
   soon get _____ — up to 45°C.

4 The way we appoint people to jobs is very, very unfair. We need a _____ system.

5 Because of new production methods, our production costs are _____ . This means
   we can keep our prices the same, even with inflation.

6 I don't like the new computer printer. It's _____ than the old one. Nobody
   can hear a word while it is printing.

7 We haven't had much work to do recently. However, we have had one or two orders
   in the past week and are starting to become _____ .

8 I don't like our new boss at all! Our previous boss was _____ .

9 We're extending our showroom by 6 square metres. This will give us a _____
   display area.

10 Our results aren't good this year. But I'm full of confidence. I expect our results
    next year to be _____ .

11 (*answer to 10*) Do you think so? I'm afraid they may be _____ !

(b) Now add any of the following modifiers to the sentences above, to give a suitable
meaning:

much   a lot   quite a lot   slightly

2.4   Look at this table for two companies, Axon and Bentel. The ticks give you an idea of how the companies compare in various qualities.

	Axon	**Bentel**
Founded in	1975	1896
Reliability of products	✓ ✓	✓ ✓ ✓
Past success	✓	✓ ✓ ✓ ✓
New equipment	✓ ✓ ✓	✓
Efficiency	✓ ✓ ✓ ✓	✓
New techniques	✓ ✓ ✓ ✓ ✓	✓
Ambition for the future	✓ ✓ ✓ ✓	✓ ✓

(a) Complete the paragraph below using a comparative form of these adjectives:

> ambitious   innovative   successful   traditional
> reliable   modern   efficient

Bentel is an old firm. Its ideas are rather old fashioned. It is a ¹_____ firm than Axon. However, customers have confidence in Bentel's products. They find them ²_____ than Axon's products.

In the past, Bentel was a ³_____ company than Axon. However, Axon has invested in new equipment. Its equipment is now ⁴_____ than Bentel's equipment. Moreover, Axon has reduced its workforce, yet it still produces the same amount of goods. It is now a ⁵_____ firm than Bentel.

Axon is now using new production and sales techniques. It is a ⁶_____ company than Bentel. Moreover, the management of Axon have a lot of plans for the future. They are ⁷_____ than the Bentel management.

(b) Discuss where you could add the modifiers *much, a lot, quite a lot, slightly* in the paragraph above.

3   Activity

3.1   *Information gap.* Work with a partner, like this:

Student B
Turn to page 143.

Student A
Look at this table of information about Mr Archer and Mr Baker. You have some of the information, your partner has the rest.

Student A: Gives information from the table, for example:
Mr Archer's salary is $30 000 a year.

Student B: Says for example:
Mr Baker's salary is a lot higher than that.

Student A: Guesses Mr Baker's salary.

Student B: Says for example:
It's (much/quite a lot/slightly) higher (or lower) than that.

Students A and B: Continue in the same way until A guesses correctly. Then switch round so that A gives information and B guesses.

	Mr Archer	**Mr Baker**
Salary:	$30 000	
Age:		37
Size of his office:	20 square metres	
Temperature of his office:		19°C
Cost of car:	$10 000	
Power of car:		2500 cc
His company was founded in:	1922	

3.2 Compare your company with that of another student. Whose company is:

- more profitable?
- more efficient?
- more successful?

- more innovative?
- more modern?
- more interesting to work in?

OR compare your car with that of another student. Whose car is:

- more comfortable?
- more economical?
- more spacious?

- more modern in design?
- more expensive to buy?
- more satisfying to drive?

Report your results to other students.

4 Language reference

Comparatives of adjectives

Comparative adjectives are used to show how one thing is different from another. For example, it may be *warmer, colder, darker, louder,* and so on.

All 'short' adjectives have a comparative form ending in *-er*.

The 'short' adjectives are:
- One-syllable adjectives (e.g. *long, fast, hot, high*)
- Two-syllable adjectives ending in *-y* (e.g. *noisy, heavy*)

Notice the spelling:
>soft — soft*er*, older — old*er*, clean — clean*er* (most words just add *-er*)
>safe — saf*er*, pale — pal*er*, fine — fin*er* (words ending in *-e* add *-r*)
>big — bi*gger*, hot — ho*tter*, thin — thi*nner* (double consonant after one vowel)
>funny — funn*ier*, noisy — nois*ier* (*y* changes to *i* before *-er*)

Remember these irregular forms:
>good — *better*
>bad — *worse*

With 'long' adjectives we make the comparative by putting *more* in front of the adjective (e.g. *more* expensive).

'Long' adjectives are:
* Most two-syllable adjectives (e.g. *more* modern, *more* helpful)
* All adjectives of three syllables or more (e.g. *more* generous, *more* comfortable)

BUT two-syllable adjectives ending in -*y* count as 'short' adjectives. (We say *funnier*, *happier*, NOT 'more funny', 'more happy'.)

Phrases modifying comparisons

STRONG   *much* (e.g. *much* bigger, *much* more successful)
                a lot (e.g. *a lot* better, *a lot* more interesting)

                quite a lot (e.g. *quite a lot* busier, *quite a lot* more useful)

WEAK   *slightly* (e.g. *slightly* higher, *slightly* more profitable)

Note: *A lot* is slightly more informal than *much*.

Comparison (3): Superlatives

(superlative forms of 'short' and 'long' adjectives; irregular forms)

1   Listening focus

1.1   Listen to the conversation with Kevin, who has just been to a conference. Mark these sentences as TRUE or FALSE.

1   Kevin thought that the conference was very good.   _____
2   Kevin's hotel was uncomfortable.   _____
3   The lectures were boring.   _____
4   Kevin found one of the short lectures very interesting.   _____
5   The lecture was about traditional marketing methods.   _____
6   The coffee at the conference was bad.   _____

1.2   Listen again. Complete the conversation. Each blank stands for one word.

JOE: How was the conference?
KEVIN: It was _____ _____ _____ I've been to this year.
JOE: What was the hotel like?
KEVIN: Oh, I stayed in _____ _____ _____ _____ in the city.
JOE: What did you think of the lectures?
KEVIN: OK. The _____ _____ was the _____ _____ .
JOE: What was it about?
KEVIN: It was about _____ _____ _____ in marketing.
JOE: Was there anything that you didn't like?
KEVIN: Yes. They served _____ _____ _____ I've ever tasted!

2   Controlled practice

Look at the tables, graphs and diagrams. Complete the sentences. Use *the* and a superlative form of the adjectives in the boxes.

1   *Students and their exam marks.*

Results in a Business exam

Jane	60%
David	90%
Tim	50%

good   bad   high   low

David had _____ marks in the exam, and Tim had _____ .

On the evidence of these results, David is _____ student of the three, and Tim is

_____ .

2   *Company cars.*

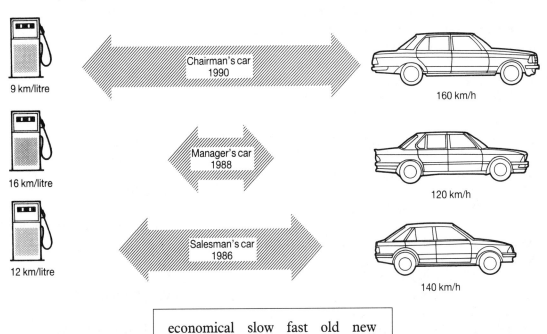

9 km/litre

16 km/litre

12 km/litre

Chairman's car
1990

Manager's car
1988

Salesman's car
1986

160 km/h

120 km/h

140 km/h

economical   slow   fast   old   new

When we look at the age of the cars, we see that the Chairman's car is _____ , and the Salesman's car is _____ .

When we look at the top speed we find that the Chairman's car is _____ , and the Manager's car is _____ .

However, when we look at fuel consumption we see that the Manager's car is _____ .

3 *Three companies.*

successful large fast profitable high efficient small

These three companies make the some products. Ozal has _____ market share, but it is not _____ company — Nafco, which has _____ workforce, and only 30 per cent of the market share had _____ profit last year. If we look at the profits and the number of employees, Nafco seems to be _____ company.

However, investors should also look at growth rates. Mentox has _____ growth rate, and it could be _____ company in the future.

3 Activity

A project. Find out the answers or give your opinion. Discuss with other students.

In your country:

Which is the largest company?
Who is the most successful businessman or businesswoman?
What is the most expensive car you can buy?

What is the most common company car?
What professions have the highest salaries?
Which is the most luxurious hotel?
What is the highest rate of income tax?
Which is the biggest department store or supermarket chain?
What is the most popular leisure activity?
What is the most profitable way to invest your savings?
Which newspapers and magazines are most widely read?
What is the easiest way to become rich?
What is the best company to work for?

4   Language reference

Superlative forms

Superlative forms are used to show how people and things are different from all others.
Here are the rules for superlatives:

- With 'short' adjectives the normal pattern is *the* + adjective + *-est*:
     the cold*est*, *the* hot*test*, *the* rich*est*, *the* small*est*, *the* nois*iest*
The spelling rules are the same as for the comparative form, except that ending is *-est*
instead of *-er*.

- With 'long' adjectives the normal pattern is *the* + *most* + adjective:
     the most important, *the most* expensive, *the most* efficient

- Notice these irregular forms:
     good — *best*
     bad — *worst*

Forecasting (1): Predictions and opinions

(future with *will*)

1 Listening focus

1.1   Listen to the talk given by a manager at Nafco. Which of these developments does he forecast? Tick them (✓). Put a cross (✗) at those he does NOT forecast.

More competition	☐	More leisure time	☐
Higher profits	☐	More money in people's pockets	☐
Lower interest rates	☐	Fewer business opportunities	☐
Lower unemployment	☐	More investment in new equipment	☐
More bankruptcies	☐		

1.2   Listen again. Fill in the passage below (each blank stands for one word). Check your answers to 1.1.

... And now I want to make some forecasts for next year. Very probably, competition _____ _____ . There are far more firms in the market now, so we must expect very stiff competition.

Profits _____ _____ _____ high next year. In fact, they _____ _____ _____ sharply. Almost certainly, interest rates _____ _____ , and this _____ _____ a rise in unemployment. A lot of firms _____ _____ bankrupt. Of course, people _____ _____ more leisure time but they _____ _____ more money in their pockets. There _____

_____ _____ many new business opportunities. We _____ _____ _____ work very hard to keep our position in the market.

Our investment in new equipment _____ _____ increase next year. As I say, conditions _____ _____ difficult, but we must hope for better times soon.

2 Controlled practice

2.1 Add *will*, *'ll* or *won't* to these sentences. The first one is done for you.

1 A: Do you think the company will hold more pay talks with the union?

   B: I expect so. But the company improve its pay offer. It can't afford to offer more money.

2 A: Mr Torinaga become the new Chairman? What's your forecast?

   B: Yes, I'm certain he be the new Chairman. He's the best man for the job.

3 A: I think interest rates rise in the near future.

   B: Definitely. And in my opinion, inflation remain a problem for a long time.

   A: I agree. There be any easy solutions to the problem.

4 A: Do you think a lot of people apply for the post of Sales Manager?

   B: Yes, I'm sure the job attract a lot of interest.

5 A: How our representative get in touch with us when he's abroad?

   B: I expect he send a fax.

   A: Perhaps he get in touch at all. He be too busy.

2.2 *Peter, a young executive is going to address a sales meeting. He is rather nervous about it and is asking Ann, a more experienced speaker, about what to expect.*

Write questions and answers from the notes. Make changes and add words as necessary.

PETER: how many people at the meeting?

ANN: not sure / probably not more than forty or fifty
PETER: need microphone?
ANN: probably not / Training Officer provide microphone if asked
PETER: Managing Director at the meeting?
ANN: perhaps come for a few minutes / not stay long
PETER: many questions?
ANN   perhaps some questions at the end / expect Sales Manager ask questions / others
         not ask many questions
PETER: expect make a mess of it!
ANN: not have any problems / everything OK

3 Activity

3.1 *Economic and company predictions.* Work with a group of students. Discuss the
following questions and see what predictions you can make for the future.

Will the company/companies you work for do well next year?

What will happen to interest rates in the near future? Will they rise or fall?

Will unemployment increase in the coming months?

What will the rate of inflation be at the end of this year/next year?

Who will the next Managing Director/CEO be in your company (or any well known
company in your country)?

Who will the next Finance Minister be in your country?

Will the economic situation in your country improve or get worse over the next ten years?

3.2 *Personal predictions.* Work with a partner. Ask and answer questions about your
personal future. For example:

What kind of job will you have in two/five/ten ... years' time?

When will you finish your business studies?

When will you get promotion to a higher position?

How long will you stay with your present company?

(try to think of other questions for yourself)

4   Language reference

Use and forms of *will*–future for forecasts

To make forecasts, we can use *will*, the short form *'ll* or the negative forms *will not* and *won't*.

The short forms *'ll* and *won't* are used mainly in conversation. The long forms *will* and *will not* are used in formal speeches and in writing.

Positive statement

He *'ll* take over as Manager.   (*he'll* instead of *he will* in conversation)
The company *will* expand.
Sales *will* increase.

Questions

Will he take over as Manager?
Will the company expand?
Will sales increase?

Negative statements

He *won't* take over as Manager.   (*won't* instead of *will not* in conversation)
The company *won't* expand in the near future.
Sales *will not* increase this year.   (*will not* is more formal than *won't*)

Notes:

1   In everyday conversation, *going to* often expresses the same idea as *will* (see Unit 18).
2   We often use *will* with expressions like *I think, I expect, in my opinion, perhaps, maybe*, to give an OPINION about the future.
3   We can use the short form *'ll* after *I, you, he, she, it, we, they*. After other subjects (e.g. *sales*) we sometimes SAY it but we do not WRITE it.
4   Notice the forms *there will, there won't, there will not*:
    There will be more competition.
    There won't be a good profit.
    There will not be many business opportunities.

Forecasting (2): Forecasts from present evidence

(going to for predictions)

1 Listening focus

1.1 Listen to the conversations, once through. Then listen again, stopping the tape after each conversation. Complete the forecasts as you hear them in the conversations. The first is done for you.

1 The builders *are* *going* *to* *start* work next week.
2 I'm sure Tom _____ _____ the job.
3 There _____ _____ _____ _____ job losses.
4 I think _____ _____ the offer.
5 It's _____ _____ _____ all our problems.
6 I expect _____ _____ the contract.

1.2 Listen again. Answer these questions:

* Which of these forecasts provide EVIDENCE? (e.g. forecast no. 1)
* Which of these forecasts express an OPINION (without evidence)?

2   Controlled practice

Match the sentences on the left with the evidence on the right.

1 The Manager is going to retire soon.	(a) Our new products are the best on the market.
2 We aren't going to win the Expo order.	(b) Everyone is very interested in your ideas.
3 Our new building is going to be much better than the old one.	(c) A friend in the Personnel Department told me.
4 Inflation is going to rise steeply this year.	(d) We've eaten so much!
5 Our customers aren't going to be happy.	(e) He left a message.
6 The jobs are going to be advertised next week.	(f) He's over sixty and he isn't well.
7 Mr Ramsar is going to telephone you.	(g) Our quotation is priced too high.
8 The bill for this meal is going to be enormous!	(h) Wages and prices are already going up.
9 We're going to move ahead of all our competitors!	(i) I've seen the plans and they look very impressive.
10 You're going to get a large audience for your talk.	(j) We can't send the goods on the dates we promised.

3   Activity

3.1   Work with other students. Do the following tasks.

(a)   Decide what evidence a person might have for the following statements:

1   Bentel are going to recruit more salesmen.
2   You're going to be promoted.
3   Our new advertising campaign is going to be a great success.
4   Ozal is going to go bankrupt.
5   The company is going to appoint more women as managers.
6   We're going to get a pay rise!
7   You're going to fail your accountancy exams!
8   They aren't going to build the factory that they planned.
9   Mr Harrison isn't going to work for Nafco.
10   The government is going to put up the income tax rate.

(b) Decide what forecasts you might make in the following situations:

1 You read that Mentox has made a loss this year.
2 You hear on the news that one important oil-producing country is at war with another.
3 Someone tells you that the Chairman of your company has resigned.
4 You find a large pile of letters in your in-tray.
5 The government announces a cut in interest rates.
6 Your boss has a smile on his face when you enter the office.
7 You see some factory employees working without safety equipment.
8 You hear an announcement about elections in your country.

3.2   Ask and answer questions with a partner. Follow this plan:

YOU: Make a forecast with *going to*, for example:
         Our department is going to close down soon.

YOUR PARTNER: Asks you the reason for your forecast, for example:
                Why do you say that?
       or   What evidence have you got?

YOU: Give your reasons, for example:
         Because we haven't got many orders.

3.3   With one or two other students, look at a copy of today's newspaper. Look at news items connected with business or economics. Do these tasks:

• Find examples of things that are going to happen, according to the newspaper.
• Find examples of things that HAVE happened or ARE HAPPENING now. Use these examples as evidence to make your OWN forecasts about things that are GOING TO happen.
• Report to the rest of your class.

4   Language reference

Use and forms of *going to*

We very often use *going to* for forecasts, especially when we have clear evidence or signs pointing to the future. Study these examples:

Positive statements
     He's *going to* be the new Manager. (I have read the announcement.)
     The company *is going to* expand. (I have read the company's plans.)
     Our sales *are going to* increase. (The present figures tell us this.)

Questions

> *Is he going to* be the new Manager?
> *Are our sales going to* increase?

Negative statements

> He *isn't going to* be the new Manager.
> Our sales *aren't going to* increase.

Note:

We often use *going to* in everyday conversation because it emphasises things we see or hear just at this moment. *Will* sounds more formal or 'scientific'. Compare:

> Look at those clouds! It*'s going to* rain today! (everyday conversation)
> Rain *will* spread to all areas today. (weather forecast on the radio)

Talking about plans

(*going to* for personal decisions; present continuous for arrangements)

1 Listening focus

1.1 It is 5.30 p.m. on a Friday evening, outside the Nafco building. Jack is talking to Tony. They are leaving the office to go home and talking about their plans.

Listen to the conversation. Answer the questions below.

1 What has Jack decided to do for the next two days?
2 What work has Tony decided to do tonight?
3 What has Tony arranged with his wife?
4 What has Tony's wife arranged to do?

1.2   Listen again. Stop the tape when you need to. Fill in these sentences from the conversation.

JACK: I'm _____ _____ _____ about work for the next two days.
TONY: I'm _____ _____ _____ _____ _____ and finish some reports.
JACK: We're _____ _____ _____ _____ for a drink.
TONY: I'm _____ _____ _____ _____ tonight.
TONY: My wife _____ _____ in a bridge competition.

What form do the speakers use to talk about arrangements?
What form do the speakers use to talk about personal decisions?

2   Controlled practice

2.1   Go through the Language reference notes with your instructor. Make sure you know when the present continuous (*I'm doing something*) is better than *going to* (*I'm going to do something*). Then fill in the blanks in the conversations with a suitable form of the words in brackets.

1
ANN: John, ¹_____ (you/give) a talk at the conference?
JOHN: Yes, my name is on the programme. You see? There it is. At 11.30 on Tuesday morning.
ANN: Ah yes. But you haven't announced the title. What ²_____ (you/talk) about?
JOHN: ³_____ (I/present) some new ideas in market research. How about you — ⁴_____ (you/come) to the conference?
ANN: Yes of course. Helen and I ⁵_____ (set) up the book stand, as usual.

2
DAVE: About your trip next week — ¹_____ (you/fly) to Greece first?
BOB: Yes, ²_____ (we/spend) two days with our Athens branch. Then ³_____ (we/travel) to the Belgrade Trade Fair.
DAVE: How long ⁴_____ (you/stay) in Belgrade?
BOB: Three days. Then ⁵_____ (we/go) to Rome to discuss some new designs.
DAVE: And after that, ⁶_____ (you/come) back home?
BOB: Not me! ⁷_____ (I/take) a holiday! ⁸_____ (I/find) a nice hotel somewhere and relax for a day or two!

3

EILEEN: By the way, ^{1}_____ (I/take) the week off next week.

BRIAN: Does the boss know?

EILEEN: Oh yes, I arranged it a long time ago. ^{2}_____ (I/get) married, you see.

BRIAN: Congratulations! ^{3}_____ (you/carry on) working here, or ^{4}_____ (you/live) in another part of the country?

EILEEN: Oh, ^{5}_____ (I/continue) with this job. ^{6}_____ (We/find) a house in this part of the city, if we can.

2.2   What would you say in the following situations? Use a *going to* form (*I'm going to do something*) or a present continuous form (*I'm doing something*). Be ready to discuss your answers. Different answers may be possible.

1   You have decided to apply for another job.
2   You have arranged to take delivery of a new car this afternoon.
3   You have arranged to have lunch with some important customers tomorrow.
4   You have bought tickets for *Hamlet* tonight.
5   You are determined to give your honest opinion at the next department meeting.
6   You plan to work hard for the next business exam.
7   Employees from your department have agreed to play the Sales Department at football next Saturday.
8   You and a colleague have bought air tickets to attend a conference in America next week.
9   You and your colleague have made a hotel reservation to stay in the Hilton Hotel, San Francisco.
10   You and your colleague have decided to visit Hollywood while you are in America.

3 Activity

3.1   Make a 'diary' for yourself, for the next five working days. Write a note of something (real or imaginary) you have arranged to do in the evening, every evening except one. KEEP ONE EVENING FREE. For example:

September		
9 – Monday Rotary Club	*12 – Thursday* (free)	
10 – Tuesday Visit Aunt Mary	*13 – Friday* meet Bill from Australia	
11 – Wednesday dinner party at boss's house		

Work with a group of students. Ask and answer about plans. For example:

> S1: Are you doing anything on (Tuesday evening)?
> S2: Let me think ... Yes, I'm (visiting my Aunt Mary).
> S1: Oh well, how about Wednesday night?
> (and so on)

Find dates when you could invite some students for a meal at your house.

3.2   Ask and answer questions with other students, like this. Use your own ideas for the words in brackets.

> S1:   What are you doing (this afternoon)?
> S2:   I'm going to (stay at home).
>   *or*   How about you?
>   I'm (meeting an old friend).
> S1:   (*answers in the same way*)

3.3   Is there anything that you or your company are really DETERMINED to do in the future (whether other people like it or not)? Tell other students, using *going to*. For example:

> I'm going to (make a lot of money).
> We're going to (win a lot of orders).

4   Language reference

Use of *going to* (*I'm going to do something*)

We can use *going to* to talk about ALL plans, but especially these plans:

- 'personal' plans (things we decide for ourselves, not arranged with other people):
    I'm going to write some letters this morning.
    I'm going to get up early tomorrow.

- Plans showing strong determination:
    I'm going to tell the boss exactly what I think!
    We're going to make this company the best in the world!

Use of present continuous (*I'm doing something*)

The present continuous sounds more natural than *going to* in the following cases:

- Talking about arrangements we have already made:
  I'm meeting Mr Nakamura this afternoon. (The meeting has already been arranged.)
  We're having our next conference in London. (We have already made some arrangements.)

- Travel (using *fly, drive, come*, etc.):
  I'm driving to Edinburgh tonight. (more common than 'I'm going to drive to Edinburgh')
  We're flying to Tokyo tomorrow. (more common than 'We're going to fly to Tokyo')

- General questions about plans:
  Are you doing anything tonight?
  What *are you doing* this weekend?

Times (2): Lives and careers

(general specification of times; career and appointment vocabulary)

1 Listening focus

1.1   Listen to interviews with three different people talking about their lives and careers. Complete the notes for each person with the correct times.

1 ANDREA

born: *13th August, 1970*

left high school: _____

secretarial course lasted: _____

started work with Temco: _____

has been with Temco: _____

2 FERGUS

born: _____

was at university: _____

joined Shamrock Electronics: _____

became Deputy Supervisor: _____

will become Branch Manager: _____

3 CHRISTINE

has been with Argos Books: _____

joined Argos Books: _____

moved to Overseas Division: _____

was promoted to Senior Editor: _____

applied for another job: _____

1.2 *Time words.* Can you complete the sentences below? (Each blank stands for one word.) You can listen to the tape again to check your answers.

1 Andrea was born _____ 13th August, 1970.
2 She left High School _____ 1987.
3 She did a secretarial course _____ one year.
4 She began work with Temco _____ the autumn of 1988.
5 She has been with Temco _____ nearly three years.

6 Fergus was born _____ 12th February, 1965.
7 He was at university _____ 1984 _____ 1989.
8 He joined Shamrock Electronics _____ September 1989.
9 He became Deputy Supervisor _____ 1992.
10 From _____ month he'll be Branch Manager.

11 Christine has been with Argos Books _____ five years.
12 She joined Argos _____ the spring of 1987.
13 She was promoted to Senior Editor _____ the end of 1990.
14 She has an interview _____ two _____ time.

2 Controlled practice

2.1 *Dates.* Study the ways of writing dates in the Language reference section. Then read the notes below and write the dates for the people below in a 'full' form. Use an American form if the person comes from the USA. Two of them are done as examples.

1 Helen (from London) — born 15/8/74 _15ᵗʰ August, 1974_
2 Bruce (from New York) — born 10/26/68 _October 26th, 1968_
3 John (from Scotland) — started work 3-3-65 _____
4 Lou (from Canada) — went to college 9.30.89 _____
5 Anna (from Birmingham UK) — has a job interview 12.06.91 _____
6 Mary-Beth (from Birmingham USA) — graduated 12.6.91 _____

7   Terry (from Belfast) — will be MD starting 27/11/92 _____
8   Cindy (from Los Angeles) — sent in a job application 09-20-90 _____
9   George (from Edinburgh) — moving to Amsterdam 13/02/94 _____
10   Kate (from Liverpool) — leaves her present job 31.01.92 _____

Now make complete sentences from the notes and SAY them to a partner, like this:

Helen was born on the fifteenth of August, nineteen seventy-four.
Bruce was born on October twenty-sixth, nineteen sixty-eight.

2.2   *Times in the near future and recent past.*

(a)   Answer the questions below.

1   If today is Tuesday 14th September, what is the date this Saturday?
2   If today is Friday 22nd March, what was the date last Friday?
3   If today is Friday 1st February, 1991, what is the first day of next month?
4   If today is Sunday 13th January, what date will it be in two weeks' time?
5   If today is Wednesday 31st March, what was the date three weeks ago?

(b)   Change the sentences below to sentences which do NOT use dates.

1   (*on Tuesday 2 Feb*) — I have an interview on 10th February.
2   (*on Saturday 15th June*) — I sent in an application on 7th June.
3   (*on Monday 10th May*) — I start work on 19th May.
4   (*on 30th July*) — The application forms arrived on 16th July.
5   (*on 7th November*) — I'm going to leave this job on 28th November.

2.3   Use the notes below to write a short paragraph about each person.

1   KEVIN MANNING
born Manchester 29/3/67
attended Northwood School 1979–84
studied Business Administration (Northwood Technical College) 1984–86
joined Excel Foods PLC spring 1987

2   JANE BERWITZ
born New York 7-14-1965
graduated from High School June 1983
BA (General Arts) New York State University 1986
present post: Sales Department, Natura Corporation (past three years)
will be promoted to Senior Salesperson 10-25-1991

3 JOSEPH CORNWALL
joined Melco Supermarkets autumn 1987
worked eighteen months as trainee buyer, January 1988–June 1989
promoted to Deputy Buyer 20th June 1989
end last month — applied for post of Chief Buyer with Luna Foods
interview two weeks' time

3 Activity

3.1 Copy out the headings below on to a sheet of paper. Ask another student questions and fill in the details for each heading. You can see examples of questions in brackets.

Name: (What's your name? Your family name? Your first name?)

Date of birth: (What's your date of birth? When were you born?)

Place of birth: (Where were you born? What town? What country?)

Marital status: (Are you married or single?)

Nationality: (What's your nationality)

Education: (What school did you go to? When? What university did you attend? What courses did you take? What subjects did you study? When did you graduate?)

Qualifications: (What are your qualifications? Do you have a BA? A Business Diploma? A degree in Accountancy ...?)

Work experience: (What posts have you held? What work have you done? Where? When?)

3.2 Work with a group of students, like this:

(a) Each student on the group writes down a job he or she would like to have in the near future.

(b) Mix the papers up so that you do now know which paper belongs to which student.

(c) Now read out the career details of different students in the group. (You can get the details from Activity 3.1 above.) Discuss the suitability of different students for different jobs. Try to match students with jobs.

4   Language reference

Ways of writing dates

People in Britain usually put the day first. People in the USA usually put the month first. Here are the most common 'full' forms:

    5th November, 1991 (more common in Britain)
    November 5th, 1991 (more common in the USA)

Nowadays people often write 5 instead of *5th*, etc. So we may see *5 November*, or *November 5*.

Here are the 'short' forms for the same date:

    5/11/91 (OR 5-11-91 OR 5.11.91 OR 05.11.91) — used in Britain
    11/5/91 (OR 11-5-91 OR 11.5.91 OR 11.05.91) — used in the USA

Ways of saying dates

The fifth of November, nineteen ninety-one (more common in Britain)
November fifth, nineteen ninety-one (more common in the USA)

Time prepositions

Use *on* for days and dates:

    On the fifth of November, *on* Tuesday the fifth of November

Use *in* for months, years and seasons:

    In November, *in* 1991, *in* the autumn of 1991

Use *at* with *end* and *beginning*:

    At the end of 1991, *at* the beginning of last week, *at* the weekend

Use *for* to talk about periods of time after *have been*, etc.:

    I've been with this company *for* two years.

Use *from ... till* for the beginning and end of periods:

    He was at university *from* 1971 *till* 1974.

Talking about the recent past and near future

this:	*this* week, *this* Thursday, *this* month
next:	*next* week, *next* Tuesday, *next* month
last:	*last* week, *last* Wednesday, *last* month
in X weeks' time:	*in* three *weeks' time*
X weeks ago:	three *weeks ago*

Jobs, duties, responsibilities

(job functions; responsibilities; advice on departments to consult)

1 Listening focus

1.1 Listen to the conversation between an interviewer and Birgitta Meyer, who is a member of staff at Bentel. Answer the questions under the photograph.

1   Which department does Birgitta work in?

2   What are the four main areas of her job? Write them down:

    (a) _____ (b) _____ (c) _____ (d) _____

1.2   Listen again. Stop the tape whenever you need to. Fill in these sentences from the interview.

1   I'm _____ the Personnel Department.
2   What exactly does your job _____ ?
3   It _____ the relations between the firm and its employees.
4   I _____ training.
5   I _____ employees have the right training programme.
6   And I _____ their progress in the training.
7   Then secondly I'm _____ performance appraisal.
8   Performance appraisal _____ looking at the performance of every employee in his or her job.
9   I _____ Line Managers.
10   I _____ the performance appraisal is carried out correctly.
11   And I _____ the performance of every employee.
12   Thirdly, I'm _____ job recruitment.
13   I · _____ job interviews and _____ transport, accommodation, etc.
14   And finally, I _____ deal with problems.
15   I _____ any problem that affects an employee's performance.

2   Controlled practice

2.1   Read the notes about the jobs of different people in a company. Write a paragraph about each person. Describe his/her job, using the words in brackets IN A SUITABLE FORM. For example, you can begin:

> Luc Bertrand is concerned with payments to staff. He deals with the money required for trips, and ... etc.

   1   LUC BERTRAND
   payments to staff   (concerned with)
   money required for trips   (deal with)
   checking expense claims, issuing cheques   (responsible)
   amounts paid out for expenses   (monitor)

2 MARY MURRAY

company canteen	(in charge of)
food supplies, staff rotas, meals	(organise)
food preparation and service	(monitor)
canteen operates efficiently	(make sure)

3 LARRY HERSCH

customers' complaints	(deal with)
complaints are dealt with quickly	(make sure)
checking that complaints are valid	(job — involve)
Production Manager	(liaise with)
write a report on every complaint	(have to)

4 IRENE THEODORAKIS

visitors arriving at Front Desk	(look after)
all visitors sign in on arrival	(make sure)
taxi and bus transport for visitors	(arrange)
messages left for staff members	(deal with)
security and switchboard staff	(liaise with)

5 GEORGE FENN

preventing crime within the building	(responsible)
checking means of access to the building	(job — involve)
test burglar alarms regularly	(have to)
people entering/leaving the building	(monitor)
doors and windows are locked after hours	(make sure)
distribution of keys	(deal with)
security patrols at night/weekends	(organise)

6 CHARLES BUTROS

health and safety of every employee	(responsible)
make a record of every accident	(have to)
accident rate in the firm	(monitor)
inspecting machines and equipment	(job — involve)
training in safety and first aid	(organise)
talks on safety	(arrange)

Which departments do you think the people above work in? Choose from this list:

<table>
<tr><td>Production</td><td>Catering</td></tr>
<tr><td>Catering</td><td>Health and Safety</td></tr>
<tr><td>Finance</td><td>Switchboard</td></tr>
<tr><td>Personnel</td><td>Reception</td></tr>
<tr><td>Quality Control</td><td>Security</td></tr>
<tr><td>Customer Services</td><td>Marketing</td></tr>
</table>

2.2   Complete this interview with a Marketing Manager (MM). Use the words and phrases below.

<table>
<tr><td>liaise with (× 2)</td><td>organise</td></tr>
<tr><td>involve</td><td>in charge of</td></tr>
<tr><td>involves (× 3)</td><td>concerned with</td></tr>
<tr><td>have to (× 2)</td><td>is responsible for</td></tr>
<tr><td>making sure</td><td>monitor</td></tr>
<tr><td>make sure</td><td>deal with</td></tr>
</table>

INTERVIEWER: So, you're Head of Marketing?

MM: That's right. I'm ^{1}_____ the Marketing Department.

INTERVIEWER: What exactly does marketing ^{2}_____ ?

MM: It ^{3}_____ finding out what the market wants and ^{4}_____ that we supply it. And, very importantly, we ^{5}_____ that the market *knows* we can supply it. So we ^{6}_____ two main areas — market research and promotion.

INTERVIEWER: Can you explain market research?

MM: Yes. We ^{7}_____ analyse the market. Sometimes this ^{8}_____ sending out questionnaires to customers. And of course we ^{9}_____ closely the research done by other organisations.

INTERVIEWER: I see.

MM: And as I say, we're ^{10}_____ publicity for our own products. So we ^{11}_____ promotion campaigns.

INTERVIEWER: Do you do a lot of advertising?

MM: Yes. For example, in our department, one person ^{12}_____ TV advertising, another for magazine advertising, and another for mailshots.

INTERVIEWER: What exactly is a mailshot?

MM: Well, a mailshot ^{13}_____ sending details of a new product to all potential customers.

INTERVIEWER: I see. And do you ^{14}_____ other departments?

MM: Yes, of course. For example, I ^{15}_____ the Sales Manager. We set targets for the sales representatives. They ^{16}_____ try to meet the targets.

3 Activity

3.1 Look at this problem, and how to give advice:

A: There's a mistake in my pay cheque. It happens every month!
B: *You should go to* the Finance Department.
OR *You should go and see* the Head of Finance.

What advice would you give if you heard the following? Study the departments in the Language reference section, then decide what the person should do:

1 The customers say our new products are unreliable.
2 The heating in my office isn't working.
3 I'm not happy with our latest advertising campaign.
4 I've had a complaint about a sales rep in our Birmingham branch. He was rude to a customer.
5 Look! This machine is in a dangerous condition!
6 My boss hates me.
7 I've had a complaint. Our service engineers didn't do a good job.
8 My handbag has been stolen!
9 Was there a visitor for me this morning? (Answer: I don't know ...)
10 Our goods aren't reaching our customers in time.

Now think of more problems in a company. Make sentences about them. Other students give advice about the person or department to go to.

3.2 Interview someone who works in a company. Find out exactly what the person does by asking questions. For example:

What does your job involve?
What exactly do you have to do?
What kind of problems do you deal with?
Who do you liaise with?

Report back to your class. Describe the job using any of these expressions:

in charge of	responsible for	look after	deal with
involve	concerned with		
make sure that	monitor		
organise	arrange		
liaise with			
have to (do something)			

3.3   Work with a group of students, like this:

YOU: Describe the job of someone you know, but DO NOT say the name of the job or department. Just say what the person does.

OTHER STUDENTS: Guess the job title, or the department the person works in.

4   Language reference

Responsibilities

in charge of   He is *in charge of* the department.

responsible for   She is *responsible for* $\begin{cases} \text{publicity.} \\ \text{plac}\textit{ing} \text{ advertisements. (Note: use of -}\textit{ing}\text{ form)} \end{cases}$

look after   He *looks after* public relations.

deals with   She *deals with* personal problems.

Involvement

involve   His job *involves* $\begin{cases} \text{public relations.} \\ \text{talk}\textit{ing} \text{ to the press. (Note: use of -}\textit{ing}\text{ form)} \end{cases}$

concerned with   She is *concerned with* the health of employees.

Checking

make sure that   She *makes sure that* the doors are locked.

monitor   He *monitors* the amounts paid out in expenses.

Organisation

organise   He *organises* security patrols.

arrange   She *arranges* transport.

Liaison

liaise with   He *liaises with* the Sales Department.

Duties

have to   He *has to* write a report about every complaint.

Giving advice

You should go to the Finance Department.

You should go and see the Personnel Officer.

Some company departments and their responsibilities

Catering — provides meals
Customer Services — deals with after-sales service and complaints
Dispatch and Distribution — sends goods out to customers
Finance — deals with money coming in and going out of the company
Health and Safety — checks for dangers at work, monitors health
Maintenance — checks equipment regularly, carries out repairs
Marketing — makes sure that products are widely known, finds out customers' needs
Personnel — deals with training, recruitment, staff problems
PR = Public Relations — talks to journalists, presents the company to the public
Production — produces goods
R&D = Research and Development — develops new products and new ideas
Reception — deals with visitors, takes messages
Quality Control — monitors company products, tries to improve their quality
Sales — sells goods, contacts customers, deals with inquiries about products
Security — protects staff and property against crime
Switchboard — deals with telephone calls in and out of the company

Some terms used in job titles

Head of Marketing
Deputy Head of Sales
Catering *Supervisor*
Security *Officer*
Reception*ist*
Quality Control *Inspector*
Switchboard *Operator*
Sales *Representative* ('*Rep*')
Maintenance *Engineer*

Meeting and greeting

(greetings between colleagues; social questions and comments)

1 Listening focus

1.1   Read the situations. Listen to the conversations. Match the conversations with the situations.

Conversation _____   (a)   An executive has just come back from a trip abroad. She meets friends working in the same department.

Conversation _____   (b)   A member of staff meets a foreign visitor to the company.

Conversation _____   (c)   Two friends meet each other. One of them has just moved to a new job.

1.2   In the conversations you heard the greeting *Hello*. What other greetings did you hear?

1.3   Listen again. Fill in these questions.

Conversation 1
1 How are _____ ?
2 How's the _____ going?

Conversation 2
1 How was the _____ ?
2 How do you _____ ?

Conversation 3
1 How are _____ ?
2 How are you enjoying your _____ ?
3 How do you find the _____ ?

2 Controlled practice

2.1 Write numbers to show the correct order in these conversations.

1 (*Two businessmen, Harry and Sam, meet at a conference. They have not seen each other for a long time.*)

HARRY: Oh, I'm just looking around. _____

HARRY: Hello Sam. You're a stranger! _____

SAM: I'm giving a talk. How about you? _____

SAM: Yes, long time no see. How's business? _____

HARRY: Oh, they're all fine. _____

HARRY: Pretty good. What brings you here? _____

SAM: Hello! Harry! Good to see you. _____

SAM: And how's the family? _____

2 (*Tim, a salesman, has come to give a talk to some managers. Louise, one of the managers, greets him before the meeting.*)

TIM: That would be great. _____

LOUISE: Ah, you're here. Good morning. _____

LOUISE: Yes, usually. Anyway, we've got a few minutes before the meeting. Would you like some coffee? _____

TIM: Good morning. Am I late? _____

TIM: Very busy. Is it always like this? _____

LOUISE: No, the others haven't arrived yet. How was the traffic? _____

3 (*Two men, Tony and Clive, meet in a lift. They do not know each other well.*)

TONY: No, I go up to the seventh floor. _____

CLIVE: Good afternoon. _____

TONY: Good afternoon. Quite a nice day. _____

CLIVE: It certainly is. It's good to have some sunshine. _____

CLIVE: Let's hope so. Is this your floor? _____

TONY: Let's hope it continues. _____

Now act out the conversations with a partner. (Do this without looking at the book if possible.)

2.2   Match the questions on the left with the answers on the right.

1	How's business?	(a)	Not bad. It was quite comfortable.
2	How do you like it here?	(b)	Terrible! I could only answer one question.
3	How was the conference?	(c)	So so. Our sales are down this year.
4	What did you think of the meeting?	(d)	Not very useful — a lot of talk, but no decisions.
5	How's the stock check getting on?	(e)	OK. We have only two more candidates to deal with.
6	What was the hotel like?	(f)	Quite good. There were some interesting speakers there.
7	How are the job interviews going?	(g)	It's great! I'll be sorry to go back.
8	How did the exam go?	(h)	Very well. We hope to finish Warehouse B this afternoon.

3   Activity

Information gap.   Student A reads the situations below. Student B turns to page 144.

1   You are a business student on an exchange visit to a firm in Student B's country. Student B is the Manager of the department you are in.

He/she greets you and asks polite questions. Be ready to reply truthfully, but politely.

2   You meet a friend, Student B, who was at an office party last night. B looks very tired.

Greet Student B. Ask him/her about the party. For example, you can ask:
How was the party?   When did it finish?
What happened?   Who was there?
Did you have a good time?

3   You have just come back from a business trip. The trip didn't go well. You didn't manage to see the people you wanted to see. Your plane was late. Now you don't want to talk to anyone. However, you have to talk to your boss (Student B). Deal with his/her greetings and questions.

4 A VIP (Student B) from another country has arrived for a meeting with your Chairman. You have only met him/her once before. You have to greet him/her and make polite conversation before the Chairman arrives. For example:

> How are you enjoying your stay?
> Where are you staying?
> What are you planning to do during your visit?
> Who are you going to see?
> What companies are you going to visit?
> How do you find the weather here?
> Is it much warmer/colder than in your country?

4 Language reference

The most common greetings with people you know are:

Hello
Hi
Good morning
Good afternoon
Good evening

Note: *Hi* is informal. *Good afternoon* and *Good evening* sound rather formal.

Common general inquiries include:

> How are you?
> How are you getting on?
> How's it going? (informal)
> How are things? (informal)

Responses include:

> Very well, thank you
> Fine, thanks
> OK
> Not bad
> So so

The same patterns occur in other inquiries:

> How's ...? (e.g. *How's* business? *How's* the family?)
> How's ... going? (e.g. *How's* the job going? *How's* the project going?)
> How's ... getting on? (e.g. *How's* the new supervisor/the policy review getting on?)

or, about some recent event we can ask:

How was ...? (e.g. *How was* the party? *How was* your trip?)

How did ... go? (e.g. *How did* the conference *go?* *How did* the meeting *go?*)

To show enthusiasm, we can answer with expressions like:

(It was) great!

It went really well!

Other social inquiries and answers:

How do you feel?   Fine. / OK.

How are you enjoying (your stay)?   Very much. / Quite a lot.

How do you like (the job)?   Very much. / It's fine. / It's OK.

How do you find (the weather)?   It's OK. / It suits me fine.

How did you like (the talk)?   It was excellent. / It wasn't bad.

What did you think of (the meeting)?   It was useful. / It wasn't very useful.

What was (the hotel) like?   Quite nice. / OK. / Terrible! / Awful!

What brings you here?   I'm here on business. / I'm just looking round.

People also make comments about the weather:

Quite a nice day; Not a bad day; It's nice to have some sunshine/rain

(Response: Let's hope it continues, etc.)

And about previous meetings:

You're a stranger; Long time no see (informal)

Introductions

(introducing self and others; backgrounds; polite remarks)

1 Listening focus

1.1 Listen to the conversations.
In which conversations does a person:

- Introduce himself/herself to another person?
- Introduce two strangers to each other?

1.2 Listen again. Fill in the table with notes to show the BACKGROUND of the people who meet each other. The notes for Conversation 1 are done for you.

Person	Background		Person	Background
1 Tom Ho	*Production Dept.*		Andrea Cronberg	*National Power*
2 Jennifer Feng	_____		Ohira Ozawa	_____
3 Lisa Fox	_____	*MEETS*	Rudi Krenz	_____
4 Herr Winkler	_____		Carl Weiss	_____
5 Ahmed Jaffar	_____		Yusef Osman	_____

2 Controlled practice

2.1 Read these conversations, then answer the questions below.

1
KATE: Your glass is empty. Can I get you a drink?
MANUEL: No it's OK, thanks.
KATE: I'm Kate Finch, by the way. I'm in the Personnel Department here. I don't think we've met.
MANUEL: No, I'm a visitor. My name is Manuel Sánchez. I'm here on a training course.
KATE: Well, nice to meet you, Manuel. Are you enjoying your stay here?
MANUEL: Very much, thank you.

2
JOHN: Mr Habib, I'd like you to meet someone. This is Ed Low of our Sales Department. He's in charge of Customer Services. Ed, may I introduce Anwar Habib of Gulf Enterprises who is here to meet suppliers in England.
ANWAR: How do you do.
ED: Hello Mr Habib. It's very nice to meet you. Are you going to spend a long time in the UK?
ANWAR: Just two weeks. I'm visiting all our UK suppliers.

1 In each conversation above, find phrases that INTRODUCE someone. Write them down. Two of them are done for you.

Conversation 1 ___*I'm Kate Finch*_____

_____

Conversation 2 ___*This is Ed Low*_____

_____

2 In the conversations above, underline the phrases in the conversations that refer to a person's BACKGROUND (job, company, reason for visit, etc.).

3 In the conversations above, what POLITE QUESTIONS are asked after the greetings?

Conversation 1 _____?

Conversation 2 _____?

2.2 Match phrases (a)—(i) with blanks 1—9 in the conversations below.

(a) By the way,
(b) who is here to look at our research programme
(c) Chief Designer for Nippon Toys
(d) We're very pleased that you could come today
(e) from the Leningrad Technical Institute
(f) Are you going to give a talk at this conference?
(g) And I'm very pleased to be here
(h) I've heard a lot about your research
(i) He's our Chief Technical Officer

1 (*at the headquarters of a British company*)

ARTHUR: Jeff, I'd like you to meet Elsie Long ¹_____. She's the R & D Manager for our new Hong Kong subsidiary. Elsie, this is Jeff King. ²_____. He'll answer all your questions.
JEFF: Hello, pleased to meet you.
ELSIE: How do you do. ³_____ .

2 (*at a conference*)

MIKE: It's difficult to find a seat, isn't it?
OLGA: Yes. It's a very popular lecture.
MIKE: ⁴_____ my name is Mike Collins, Denton Engineering.
OLGA: I'm Olga — Olga Svetlanova ⁵_____ .
MIKE: Hi Olga. Nice to meet you. ⁶_____ .
OLGA: No. I just have to write a report for my Institute.

3 (*a Japanese executive visits an Australian company*)

PETER: Now, may I introduce you to Bill Wells, our Sales Manager. Bill, this is Fuji Sakamoto, ⁷_____ . He has a lot of new ideas to discuss with us.
BILL: How do you do, Mr Sakamoto.
FUJI: How do you do.
BILL: ⁸_____ . Nippon Toys is one of our most important suppliers, and we've heard a lot about your design team.
FUJI: ⁹_____ . Feedback from customers is very important to us.

3   Activity

3.1   *Introducing yourself.*   Work in groups of three. Student A makes up roles for Students B and C. The details go on sheets of paper. The roles include:

> *Sex* (male or female)
> *Name* (a name from your country, or a foreign name)
> *Nationality*
> *Age*
> *Job* (e.g. PA, production worker, manager, trainee, consultant)
> *Company* or *organisation*
> *Situation* (e.g. in an office, at a conference, at a cocktail party, in a bar, in an aeroplane).

Have the same situation for Students B and C.

Student A hands the roles to Students B and C, who study their roles.
Students B and C introduce themselves to each other and make polite conversation.
Student A acts as 'judge'.

Continue, switching round the parts of Students A, B and C.

3.2   *Introducing two strangers.*   Work in groups of four. Work as for Activity 3.1 above, but this time:

Student A introduces Students B and C to each other.
Student D acts as 'judge'.
Students B and C continue the conversation, after they have been introduced.

Continue, switching round the parts of Students A, B, C and D.

4   Language reference

Introducing yourself

'Contact' phrases
> By the way . . .
> I don't think we've met . . .
> Have we met?/Haven't we met before?

Name
> I'm John Smith.
> My name is Mary Wilson.

Greetings
> Hi/Hello.

How do you do.
Pleased to meet you./(Very) nice to meet you.

Note: *How do you do* is not a question about our health. We can answer with *How do you do* but NOT with *Fine*.

Background (title, company, reason for being here, etc):
I work for Nixon Chemicals.
I'm with Bentel.
I'm in charge of the Research and Development Department.
I'm here on behalf of the Ministry of Science.
I'm doing a training course here./I'm on a course here.
OR we can just say our title, department, etc. after our name:
I'm John Smith, Production Department.

Questions about background:
What line are you in?
What company are you with?
Are you with Bentel?

Introducing strangers to each other

Introduction
John, I'd like you to meet Bill Cheng.
John, this is Bill Cheng.
May I introduce (you to) Mr Cheng? (more formal)

Background
... our Production Manager
... from International Computers
... Chief Accountant, Bentel Group
... who is here to look at our recruitment methods
... of our Finance Department

Greetings
Hello./How do you do./(Very) nice to meet you./Pleased to meet you.

Polite comments and questions
We're very pleased that you could come.
I'm very pleased to be here.
Are you going to ...? (asking about plans)
Are you enjoying the course?/Are you enjoying your stay?
That's (very) interesting.
I've heard a lot about your department.

UNIT 24

On the telephone

(phrases used in telephone calls; polite requests; offers)

1 Listening focus

1.1 Listen to Conversation 1. Fill in the sentences as in the example, then answer the questions.

1 *Good morning* , Mercury Hotel.
2 May I _____ ?
3 Hello, _____ Mr Lyons, Room 213?
4 Just _____ , please.
5 I'll _____ through.
6 I'm trying _____ .
7 I'm sorry. The number _____ .
8 Would you like to _____ ?
9 No, it's _____ .
10 I'll _____ .

(a) Is the call successful or unsuccessful?
(b) Which sentences above are spoken by the CALLER? Which are spoken by the SWITCHBOARD OPERATOR? Mark the sentences with C (= caller) or O (= operator).

1.2 Now listen to Conversation 2. Answer these questions.

(a) Is the call successful or unsuccessful?
(b) What does the operator say when she does not hear the name?
(c) How does Mr Wang make the name clear?
(d) What does Mr Shen say when he answers the phone?
(e) How does Mr Wang introduce himself?

2 Controlled practice

2.1 Write numbers at the end of the sentences to show the correct order. At the beginning of the sentences write in C (= caller), O (= operator), P (= person called). One of them is done for you.

_____*O*___: Hold the line a moment please. I'll put you through. (*5*)
_____: Good afternoon. International Packaging Company. ( )
_____: Ramesh Ehtesar. E - H - T - E - S - A - R. ( )
_____: Hello. This is Suleiman Ahmed, Business Training Services. I'm phoning about the training programme we discussed last week. ( )
_____: Ringing for you now. ( )
_____: Hello. Ramesh Ehtesar speaking. ( )
_____: Hello, could I speak to Ramesh Ehtesar, please? ( )
_____: Sorry, could you repeat that please? ( )

2.2 Read the situations below. Write what people say in them.

1 The Switchboard Operator at Pacific Electronics answers the telephone. The time is 2.30 p.m.

_____

2 Tom Chow wants to speak to John Omura in the Sales Department.

_____

3   The Operator does not hear the name clearly.

_____

4   Tom makes the name clear.

_____

5   The Operator tells Tom to wait, and promises to make the connection.

_____

6   John answers the telephone.

_____

7   Tom introduces himself. He asks about the order he placed six weeks ago. He wants to know if it is ready.

_____

8   John says the order is on its way. He expects it will arrive by the end of the week.

_____

3   Activity

3.1   *Information gap.* Work with one other student:

Student B
Turn to page 145.
Student A
You want to speak to Mrs Nancy Yip, Publishing Manager at Dragon Book Publishers, Hong Kong. Call Dragon Books. Talk to the Switchboard Operator (Student B).

3.2 *Information gap.* Work with two other students:

Students B and C
Turn to page 145.

Student A
You are the Manager at the Paradise Beauty Stores. You want to speak to the Sales Manager of Kindcare Natural Products. Call Kindcare. Talk to the Operator first. Then deal with this problem:

> You have ordered 1000 jars of skin cream from Kindcare Natural Products. The order hasn't arrived. The order is very important. You need the jars before the end of the week.

4 Language reference

The OPERATOR may say:

> *Answering the phone:* Good morning/afternoon, Texel Group. (May I help you?)
> *On hearing the name of the person called:* Hold the line please./I'll put you through.
> *If the name isn't clear:* Sorry, it's a bad line./Sorry could you repeat that please?
> *When the number starts ringing:* It's ringing for you now.
> *On failing to connect first time:* I'm (still) trying to connect you.
> *If the person doesn't answer:* I'm sorry, there's no reply./I'm not getting any reply.
> *If the person is using the telephone:* I'm sorry, the number is engaged/busy (*busy* is used in American English); would you like to hold?
> *Offering to take a message:* Would you like to leave a message?/Can I give him/her a message?
> *Offering to arrange a return call:* Shall I ask him/her to call you back?

The CALLER may say:

(*To the Operator*)
> Could I speak to Mr Zydowski, please?
> Zydowski. Z - Y - D - O - W - S - K - I.
> Could you give him a message, please?
> Could you ask him to phone me at 33-66-71?
> Could you tell him I called?
> It's all right. I'll call back.

(*To the person called*)
> Hello, is that George Zydowski?
> This is John Fellows, (Ocean Instruments).
> I'm phoning about ... (PURPOSE OF CALL)

Business correspondence

(simple business letters — formats and exercises)

To the student

In the following pages you can see examples of business letters. We suggest that you go through these steps:

1 Read the letters and the notes. Make sure that you know what each note is referring to in the letters.

2 Try to memorise the general layout of the letters, and the rules for the use of *Dear Sir, Yours faithfully*, etc.

3 On sheets of paper, practise the general layout of letters, with addresses, greetings and ways of signing off. Use your own address and the addresses of firms that you know. You can also include departments you know, and the names of people in these departments. Don't write any actual 'message' yet.

4 Try to memorise the phrases that are used in the letters. (There is a list of phrases in each set of notes.)

5 See if you can write the letters from memory. (Of course, you can change the details to fit your own situation, using different names and addresses, enquiries, orders, and so on.)

6 Work through the practice exercises.

7 Write more letters if asked by your instructor.

A A letter of inquiry

15 River Street
Charlestown
SD3 4BG

3 April 1990

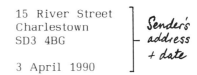

Sender's address + date

Receiver (company) + address

Informator Computers
Informator House
North Road
Port City
CI5 4TY

Greeting — Dear Sirs

Reference phrase — With reference to your recent advertisment in Computer Gazette, I would be grateful if you could send me details of your business software.

Main message

Signing off — Yours faithfully

Signature + name

Angela Jansson

(Ms) A Jansson

Notes:

1 The sender is writing to a firm, NOT to a named person in the firm. She therefore uses *Dear Sirs* and *Yours faithfully*. *Sirs* is spelt with a capital *S* and *faithfully* is spelt with a small *f*.

2 The sender's address goes on the right-hand side of the page, higher than the receiver's address.

3 The sender uses the form *Ms* (pronounced *miz*). She can also use *Mrs* if she is married, or *Miss* if she is unmarried. For a man, the normal form is *Mr*.

4 Different countries have different systems for the postal code (= American English zip code). Check on the system for your country.

5 Americans begin with this greeting (instead of *Dear Sirs*):
    Gentlemen:
and they sign off with these forms (instead of *Yours faithfully*):
    Yours very truly   OR   *Very truly yours.*

6 Remember these phrases:
    With reference to ... (your advertisement, your letter)
    I would be grateful if you would ... (send, inform)

B A reply

INFORMATOR COMPUTERS
— Letterhead

Informator House North Road Port City CI5 4TY Tel. (0776) 485014

5 April 1990

Receiver (name) + address

Ms A Jansson
15 River Street
Charlestown
SD3 4BG

Dear Ms Jansson

Reference phrase

Thank you for your letter of 3 April. I enclose
our catalogue. I also enclose our price list
and an order form.

Closing phrase

If you require any further information, please
do not hesitate to get in touch with us.

Yours sincerely

Signature, name and title

David Mann

D H Mann
Sales Manager

Notes:

1 Here the writer knows the receiver's name. So he uses *Dear (Name)* and *Yours sincerely*. Notice the small *s* on *sincerely*.
2 Notice how the writer finishes the letter with a polite closing phrase.
3 Notice how the writer puts his title (*Sales Manager*) after his name at the bottom of the page.
4 The layout of this letter is a little different from the previous one, as this paper has a printed letterhead. The date goes immediately under the letterhead, either on the left OR the right of the page.
5 Remember these phrases:
     Thank you for your letter of . . . (Date)
     I enclose . . . (a catalogue/pricelist/brochure)
     If you require any further information, please do not hesitate to get in touch with us.

C Placing an order

Northern Precision Instruments

Dell Avenue
Seaby
SB2 7LY
Tel (0342) 796745

22nd October 1991

Receiver
(title) ⎯
+ address

⎡The Sales Manager
⎢Grinder Machine Tools
⎢Industrial Estate E
⎢Cogton
⎣SZ12 4RG

Dear Sir

Reference ⎯⎯⎯⎯⎯⎯⎯⎯⎯[Precision Bearings: CG-8564-M
phrase

Please supply 3 (three) precision bearings,
catalogue reference as above.

Yours faithfully

M.C. March

Michael March
Production Manager

Notes:
1 The reference phrase often comes as a separate heading, after the greetings.
2 Numbers can be written as figures and words to make the meaning absolutely clear.
3 The writer is writing to one particular person (*the Sales Manager*). So he writes *Dear Sir* (singular) NOT 'Dear Sirs' (plural). We can also write *Dear Sir/Madam*.
4 Remember these phrases:
> *Please supply .../Please send .../Please let us know ...*
> *... as above* (e.g. *Reference as above, Address as above*)

D Confirming an order

Grinder Machine Tools

Industrial Estate E   Cogton   SZ12 4RG   Tel (0897) 126386   Fax (0897) 784036

25 October 1991

Mr Michael March
Production Manager
Northern Precision Instruments
Dell Avenue
Seaby SB2 7LY

Dear Mr March

We confirm receipt of your order dated 22nd October 1991
for:

3 (three) precision bearings   Catalogue ref. CG-8564-M

We are dealing with your order now and will deliver the
goods as soon as possible.

Yours sincerely

Nicholas Borer

N K Borer
Sales Manager

Notes:
1 Some letters follow a fixed layout, with gaps. The typist fills in the gaps.
2 Remember these phrases:
     We confirm receipt of ... (*your order, your letter*)
     We are dealing with ... (*your order, your request, your complaint*)
     ... *as soon as possible*

Practice exercises (letter A–D)

1 Read the information below and write a suitable letter of inquiry.

- Susanna Wong is writing to the Director of Studies at the Richman College of Business.
- The Richman College has advertised in the *Esperanza News*.
- Susanna wants to find out about secretarial courses.
- Susanna's address is Apartment 15, 263 Bay Street, Esperanza 1047.
- The address of the college is Richman House, 15 Liberation Avenue, Esperanza.
- The date is the twenty-fifth of July, nineteen ninety-three.

2 Write a suitable reply to Susanna Wong from the Richman College. Think of answers to these questions:

- Who sends the reply? What is the title of the person?
- What kind of letter heading appears on the letter? (You can 'design' a letterhead for yourself.)
- What does the writer enclose?
- How does the writer 'sign off'?

3 Make up letters of inquiry for yourself. (Perhaps you can write and send some of the letters.) Here are some things you can inquire about:

- Bank accounts
- Insurance (insurance policies, life insurance, car insurance, etc.)
- Catalogues from mail-order companies
- Business courses, training courses, language courses
- Holidays, vacations, tours (write to travel agents)
- The products of any company
- Clubs and societies

4 Write a letter according to the information below:

- Your address is Executive Training Services, 15 Brendan House, Dublin 00400, Republic of Ireland, telephone 01-704-829. (You can lay this out as a letterhead if you like.)
- Your name is Helen Finn.
- You are the Manager of the Training Equipment Department.
- You need two video cameras.
- The supplier of the cameras is New-tec Electronic Supplies.
- The cameras are numbered C3221 in the New-tec catalogue.
- The date is the fifth of November, nineteen ninety-four.
- New-tec is at 14 Farnall Way, Birmingham NE11, UK.

5 Write a reply to the order above. Continue from the letterhead below. Use this information:

*   Your name is Gordon Prentice
*   You are the Sales Manager at New-tec.

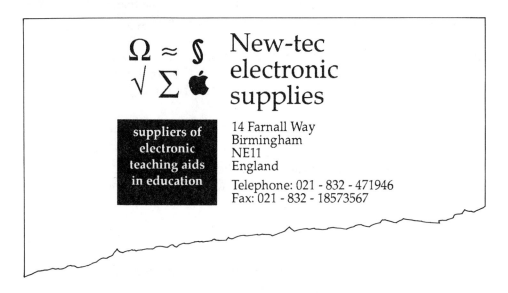

6 Write a letter ordering any item from a catalogue or advertisement in your country.

Note:
It is often necessary to send money with your order, especially if you are writing as a private person, not as a person in a company. You can add this sentence after your order.
  I enclose a cheque for ... (an amount of money)

7 Write a letter confirming the order sent in Exercise 6 above.

E A hotel reservation

Letterhead

INFORMATOR COMPUTERS

Informator House North Road Port City CI5 4TY Tel. (0776) 485014

Date — 5 April 1990

Receiver
(department)
+ address

Reservations Department
Milton Hotel
Park Avenue
Hazeldon
Surrey
SU11 4BY

Greeting — Dear Sir/Madam

Main
message

We wish to reserve five single rooms for Informator staff, from Monday 23 August to Friday 27 August (4 nights).

Please advise us if the accommodation is available, with your rates.

Closing
phrase — We look forward to hearing from you.

Signing
off — Yours faithfully

Signature — *Margaret O'Shea*

Name and
department

Margaret O'Shea
Personnel Department

Notes:

1 Women are occupying more and more managerial posts. Thus, forms like *Dear Sir/Madam* are becoming more common instead of *Dear Sir*.
2 Hotel reservations should give the number of rooms required, the type of room required (single, double, twin), the dates required, with the number of nights.
3 Notice this common polite closing phrase:
   We look forward to hearing from you.
4 Remember also these phrases:
   We wish to ... (reserve a room)
   Please advise us if .. is available.

F Inquiries about hotel rates (American format)

742–8500

2 Center Plaza
Government Center
Boston
MA 02108

```
HYATT REGENCY                    May 22, 1991
122 North Second Street
Phoenix, Arizona 85004


Gentlemen:

Tariff / Weekend rates

Would you please send us your current tariff
including special weekend rates.

Thank you for your attention to this matter.


Very truly yours
```

[signature: Alan Van der Berg]

```
Alan Van der Berg
Assistant Manager
```

Notes:
1 *Gentlemen* is the most common greeting if no particular person is addressed. Other possible forms are *Ladies and Gentlemen* and *Dear Sir or Madam.*
2 *Dear Sirs* and *Dear Sir* (common British forms) are not so common in the USA.
3 As in Britain, forms like *Dear Mr Jones, Dear Mrs Smith* are common.
4 Notice that in the USA there is a colon (:) after the greeting.
5 Notice that in the USA the date is written in the order *month, day*. For example: *June 15, 1991.*
6 The most common signing-off phrases in the USA are:
   Very truly yours; Yours very truly; Yours truly (with *Gentlemen*).
   Sincerely yours; Very sincerely yours; Yours sincerely; Yours cordially (with *Dear Mr Jones*, etc.).

G   Regrets and offers (reply to letter E)

The Milton Hotel

Park Avenue
Hazeldon
Surrey
SU11 4BY

Reservations tel:
(0574) 778463

```
Ms Margaret O'Shea                              April 6th 1990
Personnel Department
Informator Computers
Informator House
North Road
Port City
CI5 4TY


Dear Ms O'Shea

        Accommodation for Informator staff, 23-27 April

With reference to your letter of April 5th, we regret that we are unable to
provide five single rooms from 23-27 August.  However, we can offer three
single rooms and one large twin room.

Our normal rates are £45 per person per night.  However, we can offer you
a special 20% discount, hence £36 per person per night.  This includes
breakfast.

We hope this is acceptable, and look forward to hearing from you.

Yours sincerely
```

Elizabeth Durrant

```
Elizabeth Durrant
Front Office Manager
```

Notes:
1 If you cannot give your customer what he/she wants, you may offer an alternative.
2 Remember these phrases:
   We regret that we are unable to ...
   However, we can offer ...
   We hope this is acceptable ...

H   Replying to a telephone complaint

Northern Precision Instruments

Dell Avenue
Seaby
SB2 7LY
Tel (0342) 796745

George Lebrun   15 January 1992
Production Manager
Outils de Bourgogne
21000 Dijon
France

Dear Monsieur Lebrun

Reference phrase — Further to our telephone conversation yesterday, I am
very sorry that we sent you the wrong components. The
mistake was due to a clerical error.

I confirm that we are sending you a replacement by
special delivery. It should arrive by the end of the
week.

Once again, my apologies.

Yours sincerely

John White

John White
Customer Services Department

Notes:
1 Note the expression *Further to*, used to give the idea of CONTINUING a conversation.
2 Note how the writer apologises, gives a reason for the mistake, and promises action.
3 Remember these phrases:
   Further to our telephone conversation . . .
   I am very sorry that . . .
   The mistake was due to . . .
   I confirm that we are sending you a replacement . . .
   It should arrive by . . . (*a certain time*)

Practice exercises (letters E–H)

1   Write a letter to the Milton Hotel (see Letter E). Ask for a reservation. Use any of the following items of information you need:

- You are PA to the Manager of Meldon Instruments PLC.
- Meldon is the UK subsidiary of a large international company making scientific equipment.
- Your address is 189 Fenn Way, Newchurch NC12 4HJ, UK.
- You need accommodation for the President of your company, who is arriving from the USA with his wife.
- A previous VIP visiting your company stayed with his family at the Bella Vista suite. He was very satisfied with it. You would like to reserve this suite if possible.
- You need the accommodation for three nights, from the twenty-fourth to the twenty-seventh of November.
- The date today is the sixteenth of October.

2   Look at Letter F. Pick out the following sections of the letter and label them:

- Signature, name and title of sender
- The sender's letterhead
- A polite closing phrase
- The receiver (+ address)
- The greeting
- The signing-off phrase
- A reference phrase
- The main message

3   On a separate sheet of paper, show how you could change letter E if it came from a British travel agency.

4   Write a letter (British or American style) requesting a brochure from any firm in your country which supplies goods or services.

5   Write a reply from the Milton Hotel to Letter F. Use any of the following items of information you need:

- The Bella Vista suite is not available until the thirtieth of November.
- The Milton Hotel's luxury Penthouse Suite is available on the dates requested.
- The Penthouse Suite is on the top floor of the hotel. It is completely private, and has a beautiful view over the surrounding countryside.
- The rate for the Penthouse Suite if £280 per night.
- The rate for the Bella Vista Suite is £190 per night.
- The rates include full English breakfast and unlimited use of the hotel's leisure facilities (golf, fishing, squash, swimming, sauna).

6   Write a letter from George Tong, the Manager of the Sales Department, Northern Precision Instruments (see Letter G). Use any of the following items of information you need:

- The date is the twelfth of March, nineteen ninety-three.
- This morning you had a phone call from Les Archer, Chief Buyer, Exco Hardware Suppliers, 3 West Street, Homesdon HD1 4BY.
- The invoice for the last consignment of instruments you sent to Exco was incorrect.
- The invoice said £10 250. According to Mr Archer, the correct figure should be £8790.
- You agree with Mr Archer's calculations.
- You suggest that a computer made the error.
- You enclose an invoice for the correct figure.

7   Write a letter to any firm or institution (real or imaginary) replying to a telephone complaint about:

   (a)   Late delivery of a product
or (b)   The quality of a product
or (c)   Delivery of the wrong product
or (d)   Poor quality of service (in a hotel, teaching institution, private medical clinic, etc.)

Information gap: Students B and C

Unit 5

3.4

Student B
You are going on holiday with Student A. You need a camera to take with you. Obtain information about camera A. Answer questions about camera B.

The cameras have the same features — lenses, speeds, etc. Which camera offers better value for money?

Camera A

Dimensions: _____
_____
_____
Weight: _____
Price: _____

Camera B

Width: 21.1 cm
Height: 6.6 cm
Depth: 4.8 cm
Weight: 225 gm
Price: £85

Unit 6

3.3

Student B
You are the boss. Discuss with your secretary (Student A) your engagements for the day. Your diary (next page) is not the same as your secretary's desk diary.

With Student A, decide on the most suitable times and make suggestions (e.g. about rescheduling an appointment, etc.). For example, you could say:

Perhaps we can change the (appointment) to ... (new time).
Perhaps I could (have lunch) between ... and ... (new times).

---

19 Friday

Reports to write — NO INTERRUPTIONS !	9.30 – 10.15 AM
Meeting (John Boreman , Systems analyst)	10.20 – 12.15
Lunch with Gloria Fox , Femina Fashions	12.30 – 1.45 PM
Meet M.D. (about new advertising campaign)	3.30 – 4.50
Cocktails (visiting VIPs from Japan)	5.00

Unit 9

3.3

Student B
Look at the floor plans opposite. They show the plan of the Bentel Corporation Building. Ask for and give information about how to get to people and places located in the building.

Label your plan.

Ask for:
Susanna Steiner, the Finance Manager
Paul Vinson, the Production Manager
The toilets
A drink
Ask to send a fax
Victor Gonzalez, the Marketing Assistant
The conference room
The store room
International Division

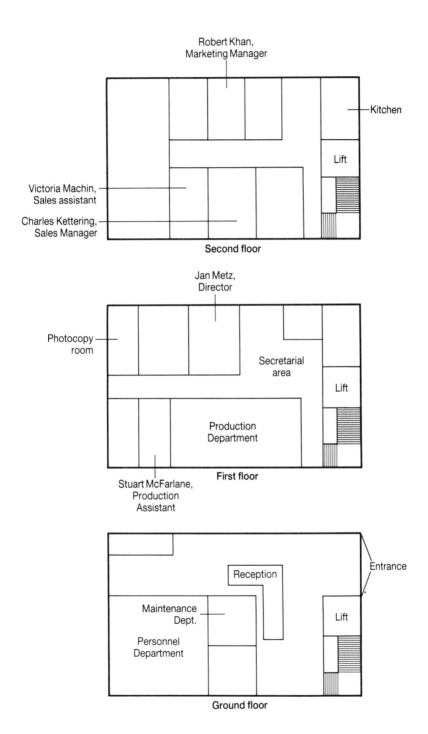

Robert Khan,
Marketing Manager

Kitchen

Lift

Victoria Machin,
Sales assistant

Charles Kettering,
Sales Manager

Second floor

Jan Metz,
Director

Photocopy
room

Secretarial
area

Lift

Production
Department

First floor

Stuart McFarlane,
Production
Assistant

Reception

Entrance

Maintenance
Dept.

Lift

Personnel
Department

Ground floor

Unit 10

3.1

Student B
Look at this check-list. It shows some of the things that are or aren't in your office. You have some of the information. Your partner has the rest.

Blu-tack®	☒	erasers	☐	scotch tape	☐
correcting fluid	☑	felt-tip pens	☐	staples	☑
drawing pins	☐	glue	☐	stamps	☒
envelopes	☑	paper clips	☒	typing paper	☐

Ask and answer questions like this, and fill in the check-list.

Q: Have we got any ... (glue, etc.)
A: Yes, we've got some. We don't need any.
   or
   No, we haven't got any. We need some.

Unit 12

3.2

Student B
Answer Student A's questions using the information in the table opposite. Try to make your answers fit A's questions so that they sound 'real'. For example:

Question: How many brochures did we print for our new advertising campaign?
Answer: Oh, we printed a lot of brochures — more than ten thousand. We don't need any more ..., etc.

Note: Remember that you can use *quite a lot* for quantities less than *a lot*, and *some* for quantities in the middle of the scale (see Language reference section).

	None	A large quantity

	None→A large quantity
equipment	✓
new products	✓
stationery	✓
fuel	✓
technicians	✓
job applicants	✓
information	✓
competition	✓
orders	✓
brochures	✓
industrial robots	✓
evidence	✓
software	✓
money	✓
credit	✓
time	✓
sales representatives	✓
expertise	✓
catalogues	✓
spare capacity	✓

Unit 14

3

Student B

Listen to your partner's information. Make a rough diagram from the information you hear about exports of cars by Northland, 1980−87. The start of the diagram is given.

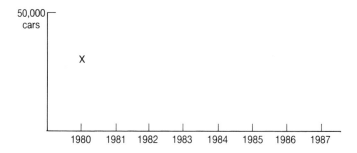

Look at this diagram. It shows how the export of oil by Southland changed between 1980 and 1987. Tell your partner about the diagram. Make sentences like this.

In 1981, Southland exported far more oil than in 1980.

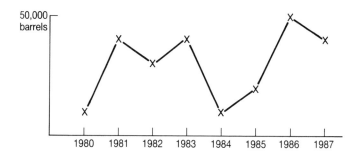

When you have finished, you and your partner check the diagrams you have drawn.

Unit 15

3.1

Student B
Look at this table of information about Mr Archer and Mr Baker. You have some of the information, your partner has the rest.

Student A: Gives information from the table, for example:
Mr Archer's salary is $30 000 a year.
Student B: Says for example:
Mr Baker's salary is a lot higher than that.
Student A: Guesses Mr Baker's salary.
Student B: Says for example:
It's (much/quite a lot/slightly) higher (or lower) than that.

Continue in the same way until A guesses correctly. Then switch round so that A gives information and B guesses.

	Mr Archer	**Mr Baker**
Salary:		$45 000
Age:	27	
Size of his office:		23 square metres
Temperature of his office:	22°C	
Cost of car:		$24 000
Power of car:	1300 cc	
His company was founded in:		1978

Unit 22

Student B

1 Student A is on an exchange visit to your firm. You are the manager of Student A's department.

You meet Student A at work, a few days after he/she has started the visit. Greet Student A and ask some questions about his/her visit. For example:
    How are you enjoying your stay here?
    What do you think of ... (the department, etc.)?

Listen to A's answers. Make comments like:
    That's good.   OR   That's a pity.
    I'm glad to hear it.   OR   I'm sorry to hear it.

2 You were at the office party last night. You went to bed very late and you feel very tired.

You meet Student A, who was not at the party. He/she greets you and asked you about the party.

Answer A's questions. Say whether or not you enjoyed the party. Mention some things that happened at the party. For example:
    The Chairman made an amusing/a boring speech.
    There was some dancing after the speeches.

Try to make Student A feel glad OR sorry that he/she was not at the party.

3 You are Student A's boss. You meet Student A after he/she comes back from a business trip.
Greet Student A and ask questions about the trip. For example you can begin:
    So, how was the trip?

Find out as much as you can, but try not to be 'bossy'. Be sympathetic if Student A is unhappy about the trip.

4 You are a VIP, visiting Student A's country. You are going to visit the Chairman of Student A's firm.

Student A meets you and tries to make polite conversation while you are waiting for the Chairman to arrive.

Answer Student A's questions and ask some polite questions of your own.

Unit 24

3.1

Student B

You are the Switchboard Operator at Dragon Books. Student A telephones and asks for a certain person. Go through these stages:

- You try to put the call through to the person. There is no answer.
- You offer to put a call through to the person's Personal Assistant:
    Shall I try his/her PA?
- If the caller agrees, you try to put the call through to the PA. However, the line is engaged.
- You ask the caller if he/she wants to hold.
    OR
    You offer to take a message.
    OR
    You offer to arrange a return call.

3.2

Student B

You are the Switchboard Operator at Kindcare Natural Products. You take a call from Student A to Student C. Deal with these problems:

- The line is bad. It is difficult to hear Student A.
- It is difficult to put the call through because of a bad connection (but at last you are successful).
- While A is talking to C, several urgent calls come for C. You have to interrupt the conversation and ask if C wants to take the call. You can say things like:
    Excuse me. I've got Mr Baxter on the line from Vitacare Cosmetics. He says it's urgent ...

Student C

You are the Sales Manager of Kindcare Natural Products. You receive a call from a customer, about an order. Take the call. Deal with these problems:

- The line is bad. You have to ask the customer to repeat information.
- The order is very important and the customer is one of your best customers. You cannot afford to lose the customer.
- You cannot supply the goods the customer wants until the end of the month.

Tapescript

(listening exercises; pronunciation practice)

Unit 1

1 A: Is this an Indian truck?
  B: Yes, it's Indian.

2 A: Are these German cars?
  B: No, they aren't German. They're Japanese.

3 A: Is this French wine?
  B: No, it isn't French. It's Spanish.

4 A: Are these Swiss watches?
  B: Yes, they're Swiss.

5 A: Are these Korean computers?
  B: No, they aren't Korean. They're Taiwanese.

6 A: Is this Russian Vodka?
  B: No, it isn't Russian. It's Polish.

Unit 1: Pronunciation

A: Where is Miss Dupont from?
B: She's from France.
A: Where are Mr and Mrs Rose from?
B: They're from Australia.

A: Is Miss Dupont Dutch?
B: No, she isn't Dutch. She's French.
A: Are Mr and Mrs Moran English?
B: No, they aren't English. They're Irish.

Unit 2

A: So, there are two really important firms in the market? Is that right?
B: That's right. Axon is the larger firm.
A: How many employees does it have?
B: Axon has 250 employees. Bentel has 150 employees.
A: I see. And how many branches does each firm have?
B: There are seventeen Axon branches, but ... let me see ... there are only seven Bentel branches.
A: What about market share?
B: There's a big difference in market share. Axon has 54 per cent of the market. Bentel has only 28 per cent.
A: I see. And one more thing. How many new products do they have?
B: Well, this year Axon has forty-two new products in its catalogue. Bentel has twenty-six.

Unit 2: Pronunciation

A: Is there a message for me?
B: Yes, there are three messages.
A: Are there enough crates in the warehouse?
B: No, there aren't any crates.

A: How many employees do you have?
B: We have 250 employees.
A: How many branches does your company have?
B: It has seventeen branches.

Unit 3

1.1
A: What kind of goods does your company manufacture?
B. It makes microcomputers and word processors.

A: What countries do you sell to?
B: We sell mainly to the UK and Western Europe.

A: What kind of market do you aim at?
B: Basically we concentrate on small businesses.

A: How many workers does the company employ?
B: At present it employs about 650 people.

A: How many machines do you sell per year?
B: We sell around 8000 a year, but I don't know the exact figure.

1.2
Q: What kind of training do you give your workers?
A: Every employee gets basic training on the job. Some workers take day-release courses.

Q: Does the company make its own microprocessors?
A: No, we don't manufacture our own microprocessors. We import them from Japan.

Unit 3: Pronunciation

A: How much oil does your country produce?
B: Oh, it produces a lot of oil.
A.   What kind of goods do your factories make?
B: Oh, they manufacture high-quality goods.

A: Do you get a Master's degree from this course?
B: Oh no. We don't get a Master's degree from this course.
A.   Does your country import oil?
B: Oh no. It doesn't import any oil.

Unit 4

1.1
1   Can you send a catalogue to Mr Hashimoto? That's H-A-S-H-I-M-O-T-O.
2   I have a message for Miss Yeung, that's Y-E-U-N-G.
3   The Sales Manager's name is Barszczynski. I'll spell that. B-A-R-S-Z-C-Z-Y-N-S-K-I.
4   Can you tell Miss Jones that Mr Mansour phoned? That's M-A-N-S-O-U-R.
5   This is Miss Jacques speaking ... Yes, Jacques — J-A-C-Q-U-E-S.

1.2
1   A: What kind of products do you manufacture?
    B: We manufacture plastic goods, made from PVC.
2   A: Is this a good time to telephone Hong Kong?
    B.   Yes. At nine hours GMT it's the middle of the afternoon there.
3   A: How do we pay for the goods we receive?
    B: We usually pay c.o.d.
4   A: Which company do you work for?
    B: ITT. It's one of the biggest American companies.
5   A: Do you sell a lot of Japanese goods?
    B: Yes. For example, we find VCR sales very profitable.

Unit 4: Pronunciation

A: What does VAT stand for?
B: It stands for 'Value Added Tax'.

A: What do the letters PLC stand for?
B: They stand for 'Public Limited Company'.

A: Britain is a member of the EEC.
B: EEC? What does that mean?
A: The European Economic Community.

Unit 5

1 *Describing a filing cabinet.*

A: How high is it?
B: Just a moment .... It's 69.5 centimetres high ...
A: 69.5 centimetres ....
B: ... and there are two drawers.
A: How deep are the drawers?
B: The depth is ... em ... 61.5 centimetres.
A: I see. And the width?
B: It's 46.5 centimetres wide.
A: OK. So that's 69.5 high by 61.5 deep by 46.5 wide.
B: That's right.
A: That sounds fine. It should fit nicely. What about the weight? Is it very heavy?
B: Well, it'll need two people to lift it ...

2 *Specifying the dimensions of a metal panel.*

A: Can you give me the dimensions?
B: Yes. Each panel is 1.5 metres long, 1.2 metres wide and .05 metres thick.
A: Just a moment. .05 metres thick, did you say?
B: Yes .05 metres — that's 5 centimetres.
A: OK ... so length 1.5 metres, width 1.2, thickness .05?
B: You've got it.
A: And the weight of each panel? What do they weigh?
B: They're quite heavy. Each panel weighs 22.5 kilos.
A: Yeah ... Anyway, 22.5 kilos, measuring 1.5 by 1.2 by .05. ... That sounds exactly what we need ...

3 *Describing a freight container.*

A: Can you give me the measurements?
B: OK. Have you got a pen?
A: Yeah.
B: OK. It's 3.4 metres long ...
A: Length 3.4 metres. Right .... And what's the width?
B: It's ... em .... It's 2.2 metres wide ...
A: 2.2 metres. ... And the height? How high is it?
B: It's .... It's 1.9 metres high.
A: Height, 1.9 metres. Good ... so that's 3.4 by 2.2 by 1.9. Yes, that sounds big enough ...

1.3 *(Extract from Conversation 2)*

A: And the weight of each panel? What do they weigh?
B: They're quite heavy. Each panel weighs 22.5 kilos.

Unit 5: Pronunciation

A: Can you give me the measurements? How wide is it?
B: It's .75 metres wide.
A: And the height?
B: 1.96 metres.
A: And the thickness?
B: It's 3.7 centimetres thick.

A: What are the dimensions of the package?
B: It's 40 centimetres long, 30 centimetres wide, and 16 centimetres high.
A: I see. And what does it weigh?
B: It weighs about 10 kilos.

Unit 6

1.1,   1.2
MAN: So, what's the programme for tomorrow? I have a planning session in the morning, don't I?
SEC: Yes, but remember . . . Before the planning session you meet the new PAs. They start work tomorrow, and you give them a briefing. That's at half past eight.
MAN: Ah yes . . .
SEC: Then we have the planning session. That's from nine till ten forty-five.
MAN: Ten forty-five?
SEC: Yes. The session finishes at quarter to eleven. After that you have a meeting with Mr Black of Itemco, between eleven and twelve.
MAN: Mm. And then I go to the Tec-2000 exhibition . . . .
SEC: Yes. You go to the Tec-2000 exhibition and have lunch there. That's at quarter to one.
MAN: I hope there's time to look at the exhibition.
SEC: The exhibition goes on till half past three. So you have time to go round the exhibition between two and three thirty.
MAN: Well, that gives me enough time. Is there anything after that?
SEC: Yes. The Managing Director of Mercury Robotics arrives tomorrow. You're supposed to meet him at the airport, at five fifteen.
MAN: Oh dear! It seems I'm going to have a busy day . . .

Unit 6: Pronunciation

The course begins at ten thirty.
We begin with a lecture . . .
. . . and continue with a workshop at eleven forty-five.
There's a five-minute break before the workshop.
The workshop goes on till twelve thirty.
After that we have a break for lunch.

A: When do you begin your classes?
B: We begin at ten thirty.
A: What time does the lunch break finish?
B: It finishes at two o'clock.
A: How long does the break last?
B.   It lasts an hour and a half.

Unit 7

1.1, 1.2
1   A: Are you writing a report?
    B: No, I'm not writing a report. I'm writing an article for *Business News*.
2   A: Is the company having a good year?
    B: Yes. Our Sales Department is recruiting a lot of extra staff.
3   A: Where is Harry? Is he having lunch?
    B: No. He's showing some visitors round the building.
4   A: Look at these sales figures. What do you think?
    B: They aren't very good. I'm afraid we aren't winning many orders.
5   A: Excuse me — are you reading this newspaper?
    B: I'm not reading it at the moment. You can have it.

Unit 7: Pronunciation

A: Hello, can I speak to Mr Edmonds please?
B: I'm afraid he isn't available.
     He's having lunch at the moment.
A: Well, this is John Rae speaking.
     I'm phoning from our Italian office.
     I'm visiting our suppliers here.
     Can you ask Mr Edmonds to call me back?

A: Would you like to come and have a drink?
B: I'm afraid I can't.
     I'm writing a report at the moment.

Unit 8

1.1
1 Hello. Mr Fisher is here at reception ... Yes ... OK, I'll tell him to go up to your room.
2 Well, at our last meeting we discussed our latest designs. Today we have Mr Long from the Marketing Department to tell us about the competition.
3 No, I'm sorry, Mrs Pereira isn't in the office today — I think she's at home. Would you like her home number?
4 Miss Connor? Yes — Miss Connor is through there ... you see? ... in the showroom.
5 Hello. I'm afraid there's no reply from Mr Renaldo in his room, but we think he's in the restaurant. If you hold on I'll put a call out for him.
6 This is a call for Mr James Cox in the departure lounge. Will Mr James Cox travelling on Flight 309 to Rome please go to Gate 9 immediately? Thank you.

1.2
1 What machine can you see on the desk?
2 Which part of the computer is above the disc drive?
3 Which part of the computer is on the right of the desk, next to the lamp?
4 What part of the computer is in front of the disc drive?
5 What are the small, flat objects between the keyboard and the printer?
6 Which part of the computer is among the floppy discs?
7 What is on the wall, above the desk?
8 What does it say at the top of the chart?
9 What can you see behind the printer?

Unit 8: Pronunciation

A: Can you bring me the file on Bentel, please?
B: Which one? There's a pile of them here.
A: The one at the top of the pile.

A: Put this report in the filing cabinet.
B: Which one? The one on the left?
A: No, the one on the right.

A: Put this sheet of paper in the folder.
B: Which folder?
A: The one on the table.
B: Which table?
A: The table in front of the window.
B: OK.

Unit 9

1.1, 1.2

1 A: Excuse me. I'm looking for the Sales Department.
   B: The Sales Department? It's upstairs, on the first floor.
   A: Thanks very much.
2 A: Er .... Could you tell me how to get to the Managing Director's office? I have an appointment.
   B: Yes. Take the lift to the second floor. It's the third door on the right as you come out of the lift.
   A: Thanks.
3 A: Excuse me. Where's the showroom?
   B: It's on this floor, through that door there.
4 A: Could you tell me where the Art and Design department is, please?
   B: Yes. Go up to the first floor. It's at the end of the corridor, next to the lift.
   A: Thank you.
5 B: Can I help you?
   A: Yes, I'm looking for the printing room. I have to service one of the machines.
   B. Just go downstairs. It's opposite the canteen.
   A: Thanks very much.

Unit 9: Pronunciation

A: Excuse me. Where's the library?
B: It's upstairs, on the first floor.

A: Excuse me. I'm looking for the Director of Studies.
B: She's upstairs — the fourth door on the right.

A: Can you tell me where the office is, please?
B: It's through that door there.

A: Can you tell me how to get to the coffee bar?
B: It's downstairs, in the basement.

A: I'm looking for the Business Administration Department.
B: It's upstairs — the second door on the left as you come from the stairs.

A: Can you tell me where the Director's private apartment is, please?
B: Take the lift to the top floor.
   It's at the end of the corridor.

Unit 10

1.1, 1.2

1 A: So, another ten letters to post. Are there any A4 envelopes?
   B: Yes, I've got some in this drawer.
   A: How about postage stamps. Have you got any?
   B: Just a moment. No, I'm afraid there aren't any here. Try the post room.
   A: By the way, we haven't got any A4 paper left. I used it all.
   B: Maybe you can get some from the stationery store.

2   A: I'd like to pin this chart up on the wall. Have we got any drawing pins?
     B: There's a box on the shelf. Or how about some Blu-tack®? There's some in this packet.
     A: OK. And have you got any highlighter pens to mark the important dates?
     B: I've got some here. What colour? Pink, yellow or blue?
3   A: Thank goodness, I've almost finished typing this report. Have you got any paper clips?
     B.   There are probably some in the drawer. Yeah — here you are.
     A: I've made a lot of typing errors. But there doesn't seem to be any correcting fluid.
     B: No, we haven't got any. Shall I go and get some?

Unit 10: Pronunciation

A: Would you like some cheese?
B: Yes please. That would be lovely.

A: Would you like some vegetables?
B: No thanks. I can't eat any more.
A: Would you like some wine?
B: No thanks. I never drink wine.

A: Shall we have some meat?
B: I'd rather have some salad.
A: How about some fruit?
B: I don't want any. But the rest of you can have some.

Unit 11

1.1, 1.2
 1   A: When did you send the invoice? This morning?
      B: No, I didn't send it this morning. I sent it two weeks ago.
 2   A: Did IBC sign the computer contracts?
      B: They didn't sign the hardware contract, but they signed the software contract.
 3   A: Which hotel did I stay at last time? The Excelsior Hotel?
      B: No, you didn't stay at the Excelsior Hotel. You stayed at the Hilton.
 4   A: This equipment is terrible! Did Tom buy it?
      B: Tom didn't buy it. Stephen bought it.
 5   A: Did we supply all the goods they wanted?
      B: Yes, but we didn't supply them all at once. We supplied them in instalments.
 6   A: Why did our agents sell the goods so cheaply?
      B: They didn't sell them cheaply. They sold them at the normal price.
 7   A: So you're back from your trip! How did you find San Bernardo?
      B: I didn't find it interesting. In fact, I found it hot, ugly and boring.
 8   A: How did you feel about the meeting this morning?
      B: I didn't feel happy about it. In fact, I felt quite angry.
 9   A: Did you write down all the details of the proposal?
      B: I didn't write down everything, but I wrote down all the important points.
10   A: Did your company show the new C-300 model at the exhibition?
      B: No, they didn't show the new model. They showed the old C-250.

Unit 11: Pronunciation

A: I found out some interesting information ...
B: Sorry, what did you find out?

A: The Manager took me to the warehouse ...
B: Sorry, where did he take you?

A: He showed me their stock control system ...
B: Sorry, what did he show you?

A: They installed it in 1989 ...
B: Sorry, when did they install it?

A: They chose the XL-200 system ...
B: Sorry, what system did they choose?

A: It performed magnificently ...
B: Sorry, how did it perform?

Unit 12

1.1, 1.2
1   A: How many employees are there in this factory?
    B: Just a few. Most of the work is done by machine.
2   A: Is there much discussion during the meetings?
    B: Yes, there's a lot of discussion.
3   A: How much information have you got about the project?
    B: We've got a little, but not much.
4   A: Have you got many overseas customers?
    B: Not many. Most of our customers are in this country.
5   A: Are there many books on this subject?
    B: Very few, I'm afraid. It's difficult to find books on the subject.
6   A: How many subcontractors are there on this project?
    B: Just a few. We do most of the work ourselves.
7   A: How much training do you give your apprentices?
    B: A lot of training. We have a very good training programme.
8   A: Did you get much help from other people when you did this job?
    B: Actually, I got very little help from others. I did almost all of the work myself.

Unit 12: Pronunciation

A: How much time have we got?
B: We've a little time before the next meeting.

A: Were there many people at the trade exhibition?
B: There were a few, but not many from our company.

A: I've got a lot of ideas for new products.
B: Good. We haven't had much success with our products recently.

A: Does your company have many sales representatives in Germany?
B: Yes, quite a lot.

A: How much advice did you get before you started the job?
B: Oh, very little.

Unit 13

1.1, 1.2
1 A: Have you typed the letters to Axon yet?
  B: Yes, I've typed all the letters. *BLEEP*
2 A: Has Tom arrived back from his trip abroad?
  B: No, he hasn't come back yet. *BLEEP*
3 A: Have you ever dealt with a firm called Atlantic Traders?
  B: I've never dealt with them personally. *BLEEP*
4 A: Have any of the office staff arrived for work yet?
  B: I think Mary has been in and gone out again. *BLEEP*
5 A: Have you heard the news about the Bentel takeover?
  B: I've just read a report in the *Financial Times*. *BLEEP*
6 A: Has there been any agreement on our pay demands?
  B: The company has agreed to a 5 per cent pay rise. *BLEEP*
7 A: How long have you been with the company?
  B: I've worked here for five years. *BLEEP*
8 A: Why has the Chairman decided to resign?
  B: He's decided to go into politics. *BLEEP*

Unit 13: Pronunciation

A: Have you taken the envelopes out of this drawer?
B: I haven't touched the envelopes.
   I haven't sent any letters today.
A: Well, someone has taken them.
   There was a packet of envelopes here this morning.
B: Ask Helen.
   She's had so many letters to type recently.
   Perhaps she's taken them.

A: Have you ever told a lie in an expense claim?
B: No, I've never told a lie in an expense claim.

A: Have you ever travelled first class in an aeroplane?
B: Yes, I've travelled first class several times.

Unit 14

1.1, 1.2
1 A: Have you got many orders this year?
  B: Slightly more than last year.
2 A: How efficient is your new production system?
  B: Very efficient. We produce the same goods, but with slightly fewer workers.
3 A: What do you think of the new company cars?
  B: They're very economical. They use far less petrol than the old models.
4 A: I hear that the company is being reorganised.
  B: Yes. It will give the Department Managers far more power.
5 A: Have there been many strikes this year?
  B: Far fewer than last year.
6 A: Are you happy with the new publicity campaign?
  B: Yes. Our products are getting far more publicity now.

Unit 14: Pronunciation

A: Does your company have many trainees?
B: Well, it has slightly fewer trainees than yours.

A: Do the secretaries do much work here?
B: Well, they do far more work than the boss.

A: Do you get much satisfaction from your work?
B: Well, I get far less satisfaction from administration than from research.

A: Does Jane's section have many problems?
B: Well, it has far fewer problems than John's section.

Unit 15

1.1
1 A: This monitor is very small.
   B: I've ordered another monitor. It will be much *BLEEP*
2 A: It takes 150 man-hours to make this model in our Atlantica factory.
   B: It takes 200 man-hours in our Pacifica factory. Obviously our Atlantica factory is *BLEEP*
3 A: How's business?
   B: Not very good. Our share of the market is getting *BLEEP*
4 A: Is the new machine selling well?
   B: Not very well, I'm afraid. We hoped that it would be *BLEEP*
5 A: Are you happy with your new office?
   B: Not really. My last office was very quiet. This office is beside the printing room, so it's a lot *BLEEP*
6 A: How much did your computer cost?
   B: Only $1000.
   A: That's a very reasonable price. My computer was slightly *BLEEP*
7 A: Are you still writing that report?
   B: I've written it, but it's too long. I want to make it quite a lot *BLEEP*
8 A: Can I open this window?
   B: Yes of course. It was quite hot at lunchtime, but now it's much *BLEEP*
9 A: Have you had a lot of orders?
   B: No. Competition is increasing. Winning orders is becoming a lot *BLEEP*
10 A: This equipment looks rather old fashioned.
   B: Yes. We really need something *BLEEP*

1.2
1 I've ordered another monitor. It will be much bigger.
2 Obviously our Atlantica factory is more efficient.
3 Our share of the market is getting smaller.
4 We hoped that it would be more successful.
5 This office is beside the printing room, so it's a lot noisier.
6 My computer was slightly more expensive.
7 I want to make it quite a lot shorter.
8 It was quite hot at lunchtime, but now it's much colder.
9 Winning orders is becoming a lot more difficult.
10 We really need something more up-to-date.

Unit 15: Pronunciation

A: Which company is older — Axon or Bentel?
B: Oh, Bentel is much older.

A: Which factory is more efficient — the Axon factory or the Bentel factory?
B: Oh, the Axon factory is a lot more efficient.

A: Whose car is more comfortable — yours or mine?
B: Oh, yours is quite a lot more comfortable.

A: Which model is noisier — the old one or the new one?
B: Oh, the old one is slightly noisier.

Unit 16

1.1, 1.2
JOE: How was the conference?
KEVIN: It was the best conference I've been to this year.
JOE: What was the hotel like?
KEVIN: Oh, I stayed in the most comfortable hotel in the city.
JOE: What did you think of the lectures?
KEVIN: OK. The shortest lecture was the most interesting.
JOE: What was it about?
KEVIN: It was about the latest developments in marketing.
JOE: Was there anything that you didn't like?
KEVIN: Yes. They served the worst coffee I've ever tasted!

Unit 16: Pronunciation

Which is the largest company?
Who is the most successful businessman or businesswoman?
What is the most expensive car you can buy?
What is the most common company car?
What professions have the highest salary?
Which is the most luxurious hotel?
What is the highest rate of income tax?
What is the biggest department store or supermarket chain?
What is the most popular leisure activity?
What is the most profitable way to invest your savings?
Which newspapers and magazines are most widely read?
What is the easiest way to become rich?
What is the best company to work for?

Unit 17

1.1, 1.2

... And now I want to make some forecasts for next year. Very probably, competition will increase. There are far more firms in the market now, so we must expect very stiff competition.

Profits will not be high next year. In fact, they will probably fall sharply. Almost certainly, interest rates will rise, and this will mean a rise in unemployment. A lot of firms will go bankrupt. Of course, people will have more leisure time but they won't have more money in their pockets. There will not be many new business opportunities. We will have to work very hard to keep our position in the market.

Our investment in new equipment will not increase next year. As I say, conditions will be difficult, but we must hope for better times soon.

Unit 17: Pronunciation

A: Do you think a lot of people will apply for the post of Sales Manager?
B: Yes, I'm sure the job will attract a lot of interest.

A: How will our representative get in touch with us?
B: I expect he'll send a fax.
C: Perhaps he won't get in touch at all.
     He'll be too busy.

A: How many people will there be at the meeting?
B: I'm not sure.
     But there probably won't be more than fifty.

Unit 18

1.1, 1.2
1   A: Are we going to have a new showroom?
    B: Yes. The builders are going to start work next week. The contractor phoned me this morning.
2   A: Do you think Tom Choi will get the Manager's job?
    B: Tom Choi? Oh yes, I'm sure Tom will get the job.
3   A: It looks as if some workers are going to lose their jobs.
    B: That's right. We don't have many orders. There are going to be job losses.
4   A: Do you think the trade unions will accept our latest pay offer?
    B: I think they'll accept the offer — but that's only a guess.
5   A: Is this new software going to solve our problems?
    B: Definitely. We've had a trial run and it works perfectly. It's going to solve all our problems.
6   A: Do you think we'll win the Pacifica University contract?
    B: Oh, I expect we'll get the contract. I hope so anyway.

Unit 18: Pronunciation

A: I hear the Chairman of the company has resigned.
B: Really?
     That means there are going to be changes in the management.

A: I hear the government has announced a cut in interest rates.
B: Really?
   That means business is going to improve.

A: I hear they've decided to have an election.
B: Really?
   That means there's going to be a new government.

Unit 19

1.1, 1.2
TONY: Well, Jack, it's time to go home. I'm glad it's Friday.
JACK: So am I. You know, I'm going to forget about work for the next two days. By the way, are you doing anything special tonight?
TONY: Tonight? Oh, I'm going to stay at home and finish some reports. How about you, Jack?
JACK: Well, actually, we're having some friends round for a drink. Would you like to join us? After you've finished your reports?
TONY: That's very kind of you, but I can't. The thing is, I'm looking after the children tonight. My wife is playing in a bridge competition.
JACK: Oh well, perhaps another time ...

Unit 19: Pronunciation

A: Are you doing anything on Tuesday evening?
B: Let me think ....
   Yes, I'm visiting my Aunt Mary on Tuesday evening.
A: Oh well, how about Thursday evening?
B: I'm free on Thursday evening.

A: What are you doing tonight?
B: I'm giving a lecture at the Business College.
   How about you?
A: I'm going to catch up on some work.

Unit 20

1.1, 1.2
1 INTERVIEWER: So you were born ...?
  ANDREA: On the thirteenth of August, 1970.
  INTERVIEWER: And you went to school in New Town, is that right?
  ANDREA: Yeah, I left New Town High School in 1987. And then I did a secretarial course for a year.
  INTERVIEWER: And after that you joined Temco?
  ANDREA: Yes, I began work with Temco in 1988. In the autumn of 1988.
  INTERVIEWER: So you've been with Temco for nearly three years now?
  ANDREA: Yes. It'll be three years in October.

2   FERGUS: Well I was born on the twelfth of February, 1965, in Limerick, Ireland . . .
    INTERVIEWER: Yes.
    FERGUS: And I went to university in Dublin. That was from 1984 till 1989.
    INTERVIEWER: You left in 1989?
    FERGUS: Yes, in May 1989. And, er . . . I joined Shamrock Electronics in September of that year.
                    And after three years I became Deputy Supervisor, . . . in 1992.
    INTERVIEWER: I see.
    FERGUS: And now from next month I'm going to be Branch Manager, starting on the twenty-
                    second of November . . .

3   INTERVIEWER: And how long have you been with Argos Books?
    CHRISTINE: Oh, I've been with them for . . . five years. I joined the company in 1987 . . . em . . .
                    in the spring of 1987.
    INTERVIEWER: Yes.
    CHRISTINE: And I moved to the Overseas Division in March 1989. And I was promoted to Senior
                    Editor at the end of 1990.
    INTERVIEWER: I see.
    CHRISTINE: And actually . . . I applied last week for another job. And I've got an interview — in
                    two weeks' time . . .

Unit 20: Pronunciation

A: Where were you born?
B: In Manchester.
A: And when were you born?
B: On the twenty-ninth of March, nineteen sixty-seven.
A: Which school did you go to?
B: Northwood School.
A: What did you study at college?
B: Business Administration.
A: And when were you at college?
B: From nineteen eighty-four till nineteen eighty-six.
A: When did you join the company?
B: In the spring of nineteen eighty-seven.

Unit 21

1.1, 1.2

INTERVIEWER: So, you're the Personnel Officer.
BIRGITTA: That's right. I'm in charge of the Personnel Department.
INTERVIEWER: And what exactly does your job involve?
BIRGITTA: Well it involves the relations between the firm and its employees . . . and also the personal
                satisfaction of employees . . . .
INTERVIEWER: Could you explain that?
BIRGITTA: Well, there are four main areas. I look after training. I make sure that employees have the
                right training programme. And I monitor their progress in the training.
INTERVIEWER: I see.
BIRGITTA: Then secondly I'm concerned with performance appraisal.
INTERVIEWER: 'Performance appraisal'? What's that?

BIRGITTA: Yes, well ... Performance appraisal involves looking at the performance of every employee in his or her job. Line Managers carry out performance appraisals every year. I liaise with Line Managers. I make sure that the performance appraisal is carried out correctly. And I monitor the performance of every employee.

INTERVIEWER: Mm, I get it.

BIRGITTA: Thirdly, I'm responsible for job recruitment. I place job advertisements in newspapers. I organise job interviews and arrange transport, accommodation, etc.

INTERVIEWER: Yes.

BIRGITTA: And finally, I have to deal with problems ....

INTERVIEWER: What kind of problems?

BIRGITTA: Well, I deal with any problem that affects an employee's performance. Sometimes this involves personal and family problems. For example, if ... (*fade out*)

Unit 21: Pronunciation

A: What does marketing involve?

B: It involves finding out what the market wants.
We deal with market research and promotion.

A: What exactly do you have to do?

B: We have to analyse the market.
We monitor the research done by other organisations.

A: Who do you liaise with?

B: I liaise with the Sales Manager.
We set targets for the sales representatives.

Unit 22

1.1, 1.2, 1.3

1 A: Hi Dick.

B: Hello Ian. How are things?

A: OK. How about you? How's the job going?

B: Not bad. I'm starting to get used to it ... (*fade out*)

2 A: Well, well, look who's here!

C: Mary! Hello!

B: Hi everyone.

C: So how was the trip?

B: It was great. It went really well.

A: Great! How do you feel? You must be tired.

B: Oh I'm OK. I slept on the plane.

C: Well, you must tell us all about it. (*pause*) We've all been ... (*fade out*)

3 A: Good morning Mr Tanaguchi. How are you?

B: Fine thanks. How are you?

A: I'm very well. How are you enjoying your stay?

B: Very much, thank you.

A: How do you find the weather? Is it too cold for you?

B: No, it's OK. It suits me fine.

Unit 22: Pronunciation

A: Hello Harry! Good to see you!
B: Hello Sam. You're a stranger!
A: Yes, long time no see. How's business?
B: Pretty good. What brings you here?
A: I'm giving a talk. How about you?
B: Oh, I'm just looking round.
A: And how's the family?
B: Oh, they're all fine.

Unit 23

1.1, 1.2
1 A: Hello, I don't think we've met. I'm Tom Ho, Production Department.
   B: Nice to meet you. I'm Andrea Cronberg. I work for National Power.
2 A: Ohira ... Ohira .... Here's someone I'd like you to meet. This is Jennifer Feng, our Branch
       Manager. Jennifer, I'd like you to meet Mr Ozawa from Tony Electronics.
   B: How do you do.
   C: Hello. Nice to meet you.
3 A: Hello, have we met?
   B: I don't think so. My name's Lisa Fox.
   A: Pleased to meet you Lisa. I'm Rudi ... Rudi Krenz. What line are you in?
   B: I'm with United Aluminium. I'm doing a training course here. How about you? Which organisation
       are you with?
   A: Oh, I work for Dynatech. I'm on a course here too.
   B: That's interesting. Are you enjoying it? Do you find it useful?
4 A: Herr Winkler, may I introduce you to Mr Weiss of our Research and Development Section? Carl,
       this is Herr Winkler, Chief Engineer for European Machines.
   B: How do you do.
   C: Pleased to meet you Mr Winkler. I've heard a lot about your organisation ...
5 A: Haven't we met before? At the lecture this morning?
   B: Yes — I'm Ahmed Jaffar. I'm from Jordan.
   A: Really? Are you with a company there?
   B: Actually, I'm in charge of a government training department. How about you?
   A: Well, I'm Yusuf Osman. I'm here on behalf of the Malaysian Ministry of Education.
   B: That's very interesting .... I was in touch with your Ministry recently about some projects ...

Unit 23: Pronunciation

A: Your glass is empty. Can I get you a drink?
B: No, it's OK, thanks.
A: I'm Kate Finch, by the way.
    I'm in the Personnel Department here.
    I don't think we've met.
B: No, I'm a visitor.
    My name is Manuel Sánchez.
    I'm here on a training course.
A: Well, nice to meet you, Manuel.
    Are you enjoying your stay here?
B: Very much thank you.

Unit 24

1.1
Conversation 1

OPERATOR:	Good morning, Mercury Hotel. May I help you?
CALLER:	Hello, could I speak to Mr Lyons, Room 213?
OPERATOR:	Just hold the line a moment please. I'll put you through.
	(*pause, clicks*)
	I'm trying to connect you.
	(*engaged tone*)
	I'm sorry, the number is engaged. Would you like to hold?
CALLER:	No, it's all right. I'll call back.
VOICE:	Now fill in the sentences and answer the questions for Conversation 1.

Conservation 2

OPERATOR:	Good morning. Universal Transport Company.
WANG:	Hello. Could I speak to Mr Shen in the Freight Section?
OPERATOR:	Sorry, it's a bad line. Could you repeat that please?
WANG:	Mr Shen. S — H — E — N.
OPERATOR:	Hold the line a moment please. I'll put you through.
	(*pause, ringing sound*)
SHEN:	Hello, Andrew Shen speaking.
WANG:	Hello. This is Tony Wang, Atlantic Shipping Company. I'm phoning about the quotation we sent your recently ... (*fade out*)
VOICE:	Now answer the questions for Conversation 2.

Unit 24: Pronunciation

A:	Good morning. Pacific Computer Systems.
	May I help you?
B:	Hello, could I speak to John Brown, Extension 312, please?
A:	Sorry, could you repeat that?
B:	John Brown, Extension 312.
A:	Hold the line a moment please.
	I'll put you through.
	It's ringing for you now.
C:	Hello. John Brown speaking.
B:	Hello. This is Tony Fox, Hong Kong Software.
	I'm phoning about the systems we discussed yesterday.

Answer key

Unit 1

1 Listening focus
1 India   2 Japan   3 Spain   4 Switzerland   5 Taiwan   6 Poland

2 Controlled practice
2.1
1 She's from France. She's French.
2 She's from Spain. She's Spanish.
3 They're from Australia. They're Australian.
4 They're from China. They're Chinese.

2.2
1 No, she isn't Danish. She's Finnish.
2 Yes, they're Malaysian.
3 Yes, he's German.
4 No, they aren't English. They're Irish.

2.3
(*for Miss Dupont*) I'm from France.
(*for Mrs Delgado*) No, I'm not Italian. I'm Spanish.

2.4
 3 PORTUGUESE
 4 THE USA
 5 DENMARK
 6 DUTCH
 7 SAUDI ARABIA
 8 PAKISTAN
 9 ARGENTINIAN
10 TURKEY

Unit 2

1 Listening focus
(a) Employees   (b) Branches   (c) 42   (d) 250   (e) 54   (f) 26   (g) 7   (h) 28

2 Controlled practice
1 are there/do you have
2 There are/You have
3 Are there/Do we have/Do you have
4 There are/We have
5 There aren't
6 there's/we have
7 he has
8 Do you have
9 I have
10 I have/We have/There are
11 Is there/Do you have
12 There are/I have/We have

Unit 3

1 Listening focus
1.1
2 UK, Western Europe   3 small businesses   4 about 650   5 around 8000

1.2
Question: *What kind* of *training do* you *give* your workers?
Answer: Every employee *gets* basic *training* on the job. Some *workers take* day-release *courses*.
Question: *Does* the company *make* its own microprocessors?
Answer: *No*, we *don't manufacture* our own microprocessors. We *import* them from *Japan*.

6 basic, on the job   7 No

2 Controlled practice
2.1
2 My course doesn't last
3 —
4 —
5 do you study
6 —
7 —
8 do you get
9 Do you get
10 We don't get
11 Does the training involve
12 —
13 —
14 —

2.2
(a) How much oil does Atlantis produce? (Sentence 2)
(b) What natural resources does Atlantis have? (Sentence 1)
(c) What kind of goods does Atlantis manufacture? (Sentence 4)
(d) How much food does it import? (Sentence 6)
(e) Does Atlantis have much agriculture? (Sentence 5)

Unit 4

1 Listening focus
1.1
1 HASHIMOTO   2 YEUNG   3 BARSZCZYNSKI   4 MANSOUR   5 JACQUES
1.2
1 (d)   2 (b)   3 (e)   4 (a)   5 (c)

2 Controlled practice
2.1
1 BBC   2 VAT   3 DIY   4 PS   5 FT   6 ICI   7 IMF   8 EEC   9 VDU   10 SOR
11 AGM

3 Activity
3.1
Education:	Master of Arts; Bachelor of Commerce; English as a Second Language; Intelligence Quotient
Letters:	stamped addressed envelope; care of; Please turn over
Countries:	United States of America; Union of Soviet Socialist Republics; Great Britain
Organisations:	United Nations; World Health Organisation
Agreements:	Free Alongside Ship; Free On Board; Cost, Insurance, Freight; Cost and Freight
Companies:	General Motors; International Business Machines; National Cash Register Company; British Petroleum; Trans-World Airlines
Jobs:	Managing Director; Personal Assistant; Chief Executive Officer
Person:	Very Important Person

Unit 5

1 Listening focus
1.1

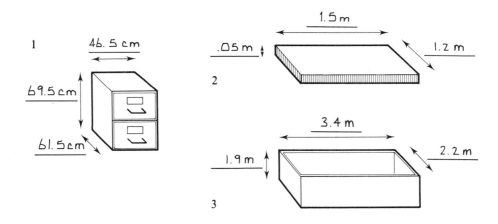

1.2
height — high
depth — deep
width — wide
length — long
thickness — thick

1.3
A: weight; weigh
B: heavy; weighs

2 Controlled practice
1 height; high; width; depth
2 wide; height; thickness; thick
3 long; high; wide; weigh; weighs

Unit 6

1 Listening focus
1.1

Briefing for new PAs	8.30 a.m.
Planning session	9.00 — 10.45
Meeting, Mr Black (Itemco)	11.00 — 12.00
Lunch, Tec-2000 Exhibition	12.45 p.m.
Go round Tec-2000 Exhibition	2.00 — 3.30
Arrival MD, Mercury Robotics	5.15

1.2
1 Before; meet
2 start; give
3 have
4 finishes at
5 After that; have
6 go; have
7 goes on till
8 arrives

2 Controlled practice
2.1
1 2.35 p.m.
2 8.15 a.m.
3 11.00 a.m.
4 7.25 p.m.
5 6.40 p.m.
6 9.30 p.m.

2.2

1 begins	2 begin	3 continue	4 at	5 before	6 goes	7 till	8 After	9 have
10 between	11 from	12 till	13 have	14 After	15 spend	16 about	17 ends	

Unit 7

1   Listening focus
1.1
Writing a report ✕
Writing an article ✓
Having a good year ✓
Recruiting extra staff ✓
Showing visitors round ✓
Winning a lot of orders ✕
Reading a newspaper ✕

1.2
1 I'm not; I'm writing
2 is recruiting
3 He's showing
4 we aren't winning
5 not reading

2   Controlled practice
2.1
1 Are you doing; I'm waiting; I'm not doing
2 He's giving; Is he talking; he isn't dealing; He's explaining
3 My feet are killing; Is anyone sitting; she's using
4 is the company getting; It's doing; We're making; we're developing
5 He's having; I'm phoning; I'm visiting

2.2
2 Miss Farid works in the Personnel Department. Usually, she deals with staff problems. But she isn't dealing with staff problems at the moment. She's meeting some new trainees.
3 Mrs Bianco works in the Sales Department. Usually, she sells goods to customers. But she isn't selling goods at the moment. She's filling in an expense claim.
4 John and Frank work in the Production Department. Usually, they maintain the machines. But they aren't maintaining the machines at the moment. They're playing golf.
5 Harry and Jack work in the warehouse. Usually, they load goods onto trucks. But they aren't loading goods at the moment. They're taking goods to a customer.
6 I work in the Promotions Department. Usually, I send out catalogues. But I'm not sending out catalogues at the moment. I'm designing a poster.

Unit 8

1   Listening focus
1.1
Mr Long is at a meeting.
Mr Fisher is at a reception desk.
Mrs Pereira is at home.
Mr Cox is in an airport departure lounge.
Mr Renaldo is in a restaurant.

1.2
2 VDU (above the disc drive)
3 printer (on the right of the desk, next to the lamp)
4 keyboard (in front of the disc drive)
5 floppy discs (between the keyboard and the printer)
6 mouse (among the floppy discs)
7 chart (on the wall, above the desk)
8 'MONTHLY SALES' (at the top of the chart)
9 some files (behind the printer)

2 Controlled practice
2.1
1 at　2 in; at　3 in　4 at; in　5 at　6 in　7 at　8 in　9 in

2.2
1 Which one; The one at the top of
2 Which one; The one on the left; the one on the right
3 Where is it; It's among; in front of the window
4 it's over there; next to the calendar

Unit 9

1 Listening focus
1.1
2 Managing Director — *see second floor*
3 Showroom — *see ground floor*
4 Art and Design Department — *see first floor*
5 Printing room — *see basement*

1.2
(*for missing words, see Tapescript*)

2 Controlled practice
2.1 (examples)
1 Q: Excuse me. I'm looking for the Personnel Department.
　A: It's upstairs, on the second floor.
2 Q: Were are the toilets, please?
　A: They're downstairs, in the basement.
3 Q: Can you tell me how to get to the fax and telex room, please?
　A: It's on this floor — that door there.
4 Q: Can you tell me where the coffee machine is, please?
　A: It's upstairs, on the first floor.

2.2
1 Fax and telex
2 Publishing Department
3 Toilets
4 Publishing Manager
5 VIP dining room
6 Bar

2.3
1 Q: Excuse me. Where's the library?
   A: It's upstairs, on the first floor.
2 Q: Excuse me. I'm looking for the Director of Studies.
   A: She's upstairs — the fourth door on the right.
3 Q: Can you tell me where the office is, please?
   A: It's through that door there.
4 Q: Can you tell me how to get to the coffee bar?
   A: It's downstairs, in the basement.
5 Q: I'm looking for the Business Administration Department.
   A: It's upstairs — the second door on the left as you come from the stairs.
6 Q: Can you tell me where the Director's private apartment is, please?
   A: Take the lift to the top floor. It's at the end of the corridor.

3.3

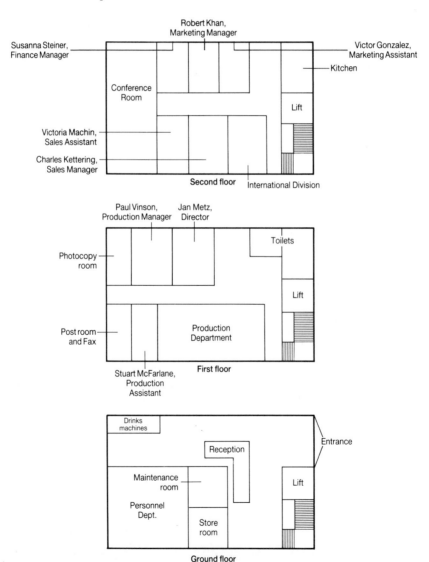

Unit 10

1 Listening focus
1.1
A4 envelopes ✓   postage stamps ×   A4 paper ×   drawing pins ✓
Blu-tack® ✓   highlighter pens ✓   paper clips ✓   correcting fluid ×

1.2
(a) any;   some;   any;   any;   any;   some
(b) INQUIRIES: Are there any A4 envelopes?
                                   How about postage stamps? Have you got any?
     IS AVAILABLE: Yes, I've got some in this drawer.
     ISN'T AVAILABLE: No, I'm afraid there aren't any here.
                                   We haven't got any A4 paper left.
(c) SUGGESTION: Or how about some Blu-tack® ?
     OFFER: Shall I go and get some?

2 Controlled practice
2.1
1 some;   any;   some
2 some;   any;   any;   some;   some
3 any;   any;   some;   some;   some
4 some;   some;   any;   some;   some

2.2
ENQUIRY ABOUT AVAILABILITY: (Conversation 1) Have you got any white wine, not too sweet?
                                                (Conversation 2) Is there any Vittel® ?
                                                (Conversation 3) Are there any vegetarian dishes?
POSITIVE ANSWER: (Conservation 1) I can recommend our house wine
                                (Conversation 3) We have some excellent egg dishes.
NEGATIVE ANSWER: (Conversation 2) Ah, no, we haven't got any Vittel®.
OFFER: (Conversation 1) Can I offer you some to taste?
              (Conversation 2) Shall I bring some bottles — two or three perhaps?
SUGGESTION: (Conversation 2) ... perhaps you would like some Perrier®.
                        (Conversation 4) How about some cheese? Shall we have some?

Unit 11

1 Listening focus
1.1
2 TRUE   3 FALSE   4 TRUE   5 FALSE   6 FALSE   7 FALSE   8 TRUE   9 TRUE
10 FALSE

1.2
3	Did I stay?	You didn't stay	You stayed
4	Did Tom buy?	Tom didn't buy	Stephen bought
5	Did we supply?	We didn't supply	We supplied
6	Did our agents sell?	They didn't sell	They sold
7	Did you find?	I didn't find	I found
8	Did you feel?	I didn't feel	I felt
9	Did you write?	I didn't write	I wrote
10	Did your company show?	They didn't show	They showed

REGULAR VERBS: sign, stay, supply, show
IRREGULAR VERBS: send, buy, sell, find, feel, write

2 Controlled practice
2.1
2	—	10	—
3	—	11	I didn't make
4	did you think	12	Did you meet
5	—	13	I didn't manage
6	—	14	—
7	—	15	—
8	Did you discuss	16	did you get
9	—	17	—

2.2
2 did he take
3 did he show
4 did they install
5 did they choose
6 did it perform
7 did they give
8 did they connect
9 did he recommend

3 Activity
3.3
2 flew — fly   3 taught — teach   4 sold — sell   5 bought — buy   6 sent — send
7 meant — mean   8 began — begin   9 drove — drive   10 paid — pay   11 lost — lose
12 read — read   13 grew — grow   14 wrote — write   15 thought — think   16 made — make
17 came — come   18 spoke — speak   19 rose — rise   20 beat — beat

Unit 12

1 Listening focus
1.1
2 discussion — a large quantity
3 information - a small quantity
4 overseas customers — a small quantity
5 books — a small quantity
6 subcontractors — a small quantity
7 training — a large quantity
8 help from others — a small quantity

1.2
2 a lot
3 little; much
4 many
5 few
6 a few
7 a lot
8 little

2 Controlled practice
2.1
1 much; a little
2 many; a few; many
3 a lot of; much
4 many; a lot
5 much; very little
6 a lot of; very few

2.2
1 many; much
2 a lot of; a few/a lot of
3 many; a lot of
4 much; very few
5 a few; many
6 very little
7 a little
8 a lot of; many
9 much; a lot
10 a lot of; much

3 Activity
3.1
(c) PLURAL WORDS: new products, technicians, job applicants, orders, brochures, industrial robots, representatives, catalogues

UNCOUNTABLE WORDS: equipment, stationery, fuel, information, competition, evidence, software, money, credit, time, expertise, spare capacity

Unit 13

1 Listening focus
1.1
Conversation 2(f)   Conversation 3(a)   Conversation 4(b)   Conversation 5(h)   Conversation 6(g)
Conversation 7(c)   Conversation 8(d)

1.2
3 I've never dealt with them personally. But I believe they're very reliable.
4 I think Mary has been in and out again. There's her briefcase on the desk.
5 I've just read a report in the *Financial Times*. The news is really astonishing!
6 The company has agreed to a 5 per cent pay rise. But it refuses to accept a shorter working week.
7 I've worked here for five years. I like it here.
8 He's decided to go into politics. He has a lot of friends in the government.

2 Controlled practice
1 Has anyone seen; haven't seen; 've just spoken.
2 have you done; haven't got; 've finished; 've started
3 have been; has changed; Has he reorganised; have left
4 Have you taken; haven't touched; haven't sent; someone has taken; She's had; she's taken

3 Activities
3:1 (examples)
   1 We've developed a lot of new products.
   2 We've decided to go on strike.
   3 Bentel Corporation has gone out of business.
   4 The meeting hasn't started yet.
   5 Our Head of Sales hasn't performed well this year.
   6 The new trainee has learned very quickly.
   7 Our sales campaign has been a complete failure.
   8 We haven't received the catalogues from the printers.
   9 Mary hasn't left the office yet.
  10 Mentel has merged with Nafco.

Unit 14

1 Listening focus
1.1
workers −
petrol −
power +
strikes −
publicity +

1.2
1 slightly more
2 slightly fewer
3 far less
4 far more
5 far fewer
6 far more

2 Controlled practice
2.1
2 Harry has far fewer customers than Tom.
3 Your company has slightly more trainees than mine.
4 The boss here does far less work than the secretaries.
5 I get far more satisfaction from research than from administration.
6 John's section has far more problems than Jane's section.
7 The Production Department has slightly fewer computers than the Sales Department.

2.2

Eastland produces: slightly more cars/slightly more oil/far fewer computers/far less steel/slightly fewer microwave ovens/slightly more rubber/far less gold than Westland.

Westland produces: slighly fewer cars/slightly less oil/far more computers/far more steel/slightly more microwave ovens/slightly less rubber/far more gold than Eastland.

Unit 15

1 Listening focus
1.1
3 smaller   4 more successful   5 noisier   6 more expensive   7 shorter   8 colder
9 more difficult   10 more up-to-date

1.2
Comparison with *-er*: 'short' adjectives (one-syllable adjectives and a few two-syllable adjectives)
Comparison with *more*: 'long' adjectives (most two-syllable adjectives and all adjectives of more than two syllables)

2 Controlled practice
2.1
2 *enthusiastic* — more enthusiastic management
3 *innovative* — more innovative methods
4 *tough* — tougher bargaining
5 *happy* — a happier workforce
6 *impressive* — a more impressive performance
7 *cheap* — a cheaper model
8 *economical* — more economical fuel consumption
9 *unpredictable* — a more unpredictable situation
10 *fierce* — fiercer competition
11 *high* — higher interest rates
12 *healthy* — healthier profits

2.2
1 hotter   2 weaker   3 cleaner   4 easier   5 older   6 thicker   7 simpler   8 happier

2.3 (Note: the modifiers in brackets are those which can be inserted in task (b); more than one modifier may be acceptable.)
1 (slightly) heavier
2 (slightly/quite a lot) lighter
3 (much/a lot) hotter
4 (much) fairer
5 (much/ a lot/quite a lot/slightly) lower
6 (much/a lot) noisier
7 (quite a lot/slightly) busier

8   (much/a lot) nicer
9   (slightly) larger
10   (much/a lot/quite a lot) better
11   (much/a lot/quite a lot/slightly) worse

2.4 (Note: The modifiers in brackets can be inserted before the comparative forms in task (b); more than one answer may be possible.)
1   (much/slightly) more traditional
2   (slightly) more reliable
3   (much) more successful
4   (quite a lot/a lot/much) more modern
5   (much) more efficient
6   (much) more innovative
7   (much/a lot/quite a lot) more ambitious

Unit 16

1 Listening focus
1.1
1 TRUE   2 FALSE   3 FALSE   4 TRUE   5 FALSE   6 TRUE

1.2
the best conference
the most comfortable hotel
shortest lecture; most interesting
the latest developments
the worst coffee

2 Controlled practice
2.1
1   the highest; the lowest; the best; the worst
2   the newest; the oldest; the fastest; the slowest; the most economical
3   the largest; the most profitable; the smallest; the highest; the most efficient; the fastest; the most successful

Unit 17

1 Listening focus
1.1
More competition ✔
Higher profits ✗
Lower interest rates ✗
Lower unemployment ✗
More bankruptcies ✔
More leisure time ✔
More money in people's pockets ✗
Fewer business opportunities ✔
More investment in new equipment ✗

1.2
(*For answers, see tapescript*)

2 Controlled practice

2.1

1 A: Do you think the company *will* hold ...
  B: But the company *won't* improve ...
2 A: *Will* Mr Torinago become ...
  B: I'm certain he*'ll* be ...
3 A: I think interest rates *will* rise ...
  B: ... And in my opinion, inflation *will* remain a problem ...
  A: ... There *won't* be any easy solutions ...
4 A: Do you think a lot of people *will* apply ...
  B: ... the job *will* attract ...
5 A: How *will* our representative get in touch ...
  B: I expect he*'ll* send a fax.
  A: Perhaps he *won't* get in touch at all. He*'ll* be too busy.

2.2 (examples; other answers are possible)

PETER: How many people will there be at the meeting?
ANN: I'm not sure. But there probably won't be more than forty or fifty.
PETER; Will I need a microphone?
ANN: You probably won't need a microphone. But the Training Officer will provide a microphone if you ask him.
PETER: Will the Managing Director be at the meeting?
ANN: Perhaps he'll come for a few minutes. But he won't stay long.
PETER: Will there be many questions?
ANN: Perhaps there'll be some questions at the end. I expect the Sales Manager will ask some questions. But the others probably won't ask many questions.
PETER: I expect I'll make a mess of it!
ANN: Oh, you won't have any problems. Everything will be OK.

Unit 18

1 Listening focus

1.1

2 will get
3 are going to be
4 they'll accept
5 going to solve
6 we'll get

1.2

EVIDENCE: Forecasts 1, 3, 5
OPINION (without evidence): Forecasts 2, 4, 6

2 Controlled practice

1(f)   2(g)   3(i)   4(h)   5(j)   6(c)   7(e)   8(d)   9(a)   10(b)

Unit 19

1 Listening focus
1.1
1 Jack has decided to forget about work for the next two days.
2 Tony has decided to finish some reports.
3 Tony has arranged to look after the children.
4 Tony's wife has arranged to play in a bridge competition.

1.2
1 going to forget
2 going to stay at home
3 having some friends round
4 looking after the children
5 is playing

2 Controlled practice
2.1
1 1 are you giving   2 are you going to talk   3 I'm going to present   4 are you coming
   5 are setting

2 1 are you flying   2 we're spending   3 we're travelling   4 are you staying   5 we're going
   6 are you coming   7 I'm going to take   8 I'm going to find

3 1 I'm taking   2 I'm getting   3 Are you going to carry on   4 are you going to live
   5 I'm going to continue   7 We're going to find

2.2 (examples)
1   I'm going to apply for another job.
2   I'm getting a new car this afternoon.
3   I'm having lunch with some important customers tomorrow.
4   I'm going to *Hamlet* tonight.
5   I'm going to give my honest opinion at the meeting.
6   I'm going to work hard for the exam.
7   We're playing the Sales Department next Saturday.
8   We're flying to America next week.
9   We're staying at the Hilton, San Francisco.
10 We're going to visit Hollywood while we're in America.

Unit 20

1 Listening focus
1.1
1 ANDREA
born: 13th August, 1970
left high school: 1987
secretarial course lasted: one year
started work with Temco: Autumn 1988
has been with Temco: nearly three years

2 FERGUS
born: 12th February, 1965
was at university: 1984–89
joined Shamrock Electronics: September 1989
became Deputy Supervisor: 1992
will become Branch Manager: 22nd November

3 CHRISTINE
has been with Argos Books: five years
joined Argos Books: spring 1987
moved to Overseas Division: March 1989
was promoted to Senior Editor: end of 1990
applied for another job: last week

1.2
1 on   2 in   3 for   4 in   5 for   6 on   7 from; till   8 in   9 in   10 next   11 for
12 in   13 at   14 in; weeks'

2 Controlled practice
2.1
3   3rd March, 1965
4   September 30th, 1989
5   12th June, 1991
6   December 6th, 1991
7   27th November, 1992
8   September 20th, 1990
9   13th February, 1994
10 31st January, 1992

2.2
(a) 1   18th September
     2   15th March
     3   Friday, 1st March
     4   27th January
     5   10th March
(b) 1   I have an interview next Wednesday.
     2   I sent in an application last Friday.
     3   I start work next Wednesday. (OR a week on Wednesday)
     4   The application forms arrived two weeks ago.
     5   I'm going to leave this job in three weeks' time.

2.3 (suggested answers)
1   Kevin Manning was born on 29th March, 1967. He attended Northwood School from 1979 till 1984 and studied Business Administration at Northwood Technical College from 1984 till 1986. He joined Excel Foods PLC in the spring of 1987.

2   Jane Berwitz was born in New York on July 14th, 1965. She graduated from High School in June 1983 and got a BA in General Arts from New York State University in 1986. For the past three years she has worked in the Sales Department of Natura Corporation. She will be promoted to Senior Salesperson on October 25th, 1991.

3   Joseph Cornwall joined Melco Supermarkets in the autumn of 1987. He worked for eighteen months as a trainee buyer, from January 1988 till June 1989. He was promoted to Deputy Buyer on 20th June, 1989. At the end of last month he applied for the post of Chief Buyer with Luna Foods, and he has an interview in two weeks' time.

Unit 21

1 Listening focus
1.1
1 Birgitta works in the Personnel Department.
2 The four main areas are: (a) training   (b) performance appraisal   (c) job recruitment
   (d) problems

1.2
1 in charge of   2 involve   3 involves   4 look after   5 make sure that   6 monitor
7 concerned with   8 involves   9 liaise with   10 make sure that   11 monitor
12 responsible for   13 organise; arrange   14 have to   15 deal with

2 Controlled practice
2.1
1 Luc Bertrand is concerned with payments to staff. He deals with the money required for trips. He is responsible for checking expense claims and issuing cheques, and he monitors the amounts paid out in expenses.

2 Mary Murray is in charge of the company canteen. She organises food supplies, staff rotas and meals. She monitors food preparation and service, and makes sure that the canteen operates efficiently.

3 Larry Hersch deals with customers' complaints, and makes sure that the complaints are dealt with quickly. His job involves checking that the complaints are valid. He liaises with the Production Manager. He has to write a report on every complaint.

4 Irene Theodorakis looks after visitors arriving at the Front Desk. She makes sure that all visitors sign in on arrival. She arranges taxi and bus transport for visitors. She deals with messages left for staff members, and liaises with security and switchboard staff.

5 George Fenn is responsible for preventing crime within the building. His job involves checking means of access to the building. He has to test burglar alarms regularly, and he monitors people entering and leaving the building. He makes sure that doors and windows are locked after hours, and he deals with the distribution of keys. He organises security patrols at night and at weekends.

6 Charles Butros is responsible for the health and safety of every employee. He has to make a record of every accident, and he monitors the accident rate in the firm. His job involves inspecting machines and equipment. He organises training in safety and first aid, and he arranges talks on safety.

Departments
1 Luc Bertrand — Finance
2 Mary Murray — Catering
3 Larry Hersch — Customer Services
4 Irene Theodorakis — Reception
5 George Fenn — Security
6 Charles Butros — Health and Safety

2.2
1 in charge of   2 involve   3 involves   4 making sure   5 make sure   6 deal with   7 have to
8 involves   9 monitor   10 concerned with   11 organise   12 is responsible for   13 involves
14 liaise with   15 liaise with   16 have to

Unit 22

1 Listening focus
1.1
Conversation 2 — Situation (a)
Conversation 3 — Situation (b)
Conversation 1 — Situation (c)

1.2
Greetings: Hello; Hi; Good morning

1.3
Conversation 1: 1 things 2 job
Conversation 2: 1 trip 2 feel
Conversation 3: 1 you 2 stay 3 weather

2 Controlled practice
2.1
1 (1) SAM: Hello! Harry! Good to see you.
  (2) HARRY: Hello Sam. You're a stranger!
  (3) SAM: Yes, long time no see. How's business?
  (4) HARRY: Pretty good. What brings you here?
  (5) SAM: I'm giving a talk. How about you?
  (6) HARRY: Oh, I'm just looking around.
  (7) SAM: And how's the family?
  (8) HARRY: Oh, they're all fine.

2 (1) LOUISE: Ah, you're here. Good morning.
  (2) TIM: Good morning. Am I late?
  (3) LOUISE: No, the others haven't arrived yet. How was the traffic?
  (4) TIM: Very busy. Is it always like this?
  (5) LOUISE: Yes, usually. Anyway, we've got a few minutes before the meeting. Would you like some coffee?
  (6) TIM: That would be great.

3 (1) CLIVE: Good afternoon.
  (2) TONY: Good afternoon. Quite a nice day.
  (3) CLIVE: It certainly is. It's good to have some sunshine.
  (4) TONY: Let's hope it continues.
  (5) CLIVE: Let's hope so. Is this your floor?
  (6) TONY: No, I go up to the seventh floor.

2.2
1(c) 2(g) 3(f) 4(d) 5(h) 6(a) 7(e) 8(b)

Unit 23

1 Listening focus
1.1
One person introduces himself/herself to another person: Conversations 1, 3 5
One person introduces two strangers to each other: Conversations 2, 4

1.2

Person	Background		Person	Background
1 Tom Ho	*Production Dept.*		Andrea Cronberg	*National Power*
2 Jennifer Feng	*Branch Manager*		Ohira Ozawa	*Tony Electronics*
3 Lisa Fox	*United Aluminium*	*MEETS*	Rudi Krenz	*Dynatech*
4 Herr Winkler	*Eng., European Machines*		Carl Weiss	*R&D Section*
5 Ahmed Jaffar	*Jordan, Gov. Dept.*		Yusuf Osman	*Malaysia, Min. Education*

2 Controlled practice
2.1
1 Conversation 1: My name is Manuel Sanchez.
   Conversation 2: May I introduce Anwar Habib.

2 BACKGROUND: I'm in the Personnel Department here.
   I'm a visitor.
   I'm here on a training course.
   of our Sales Department
   He's in charge of Customer Services.
   of Gulf Enterprises
   who is here to meet suppliers in England

3 POLITE QUESTIONS: Conversation 1: Are you enjoying your stay here?
   Conversation 2: Are you going to spend a long time in the UK?

2.2
1 1(b) 2(i) 3(h)
2 4(a) 5(e) 6(f)
3 7(c) 8(d) 9(g)

Unit 24

1 Listening focus
1.1
2 help you
3 could I speak to
4 hold the line a moment
5 put you
6 to connect you
7 is engaged
8 hold
9 all right
10 call back

(a) The call is unsuccessful.
(b) 1 — O   2 — O   3 — C   4 — O   5 — O   6 — O   7 — O   8 — O   9 — C
     10 — C

1.2
(a) The call is successful.
(b) Sorry, it's bad line. Could you repeat that please?
(c) He repeats the name, and spells it out.
(d) Hello, Andrew Shen speaking.
(e) This is Tony Wang, Atlantic Shipping Company.

2 Controlled practice
2.1
The conversation, in order, goes as follows:
O: Good afternoon. International Packaging Company. (1)
C: Hello, could I speak to Ramesh Ehtesar, please. (2)
O: Sorry, could you repeat that please? (3)
C: Ramesh Ehtesar. E — H — T — E — S — A — R. (4)

O: Hold the line a moment please. I'll put you through.   (5)
O: Ringing for you now.   (6)
P: Hello. Ramesh Ehtesar speaking.   (7)
C: Hello. This is Suleiman Ahmed, Business Training Services. I'm phoning about the training programme
      we discussed last week.   (8)

2.2 (example answers: other phrases are possible)
1   Good afternoon. Pacific Electronics. May I help you?
2   Hello, could I speak to John Omura, Sales Department, please?
3   Sorry, could you repeat that?
4   John Omura, O — M — U — R — A.
5   Hold the line a moment, please. I'll put you through.
6   Hello, John Omura speaking.
7   Hello. This is Tom Chow. I'm phoning about the order I placed six weeks ago. Is it ready yet?
8   Yes, it's on its way. I expect it will arrive by the end of this week.

APPENDIX IV

Words and phrases

The numbers in brackets refer to the unit (including the tapescript) in which these words are first mentioned. You can write the translations of the words in your own language.

absence (from work) (12)
accountancy (3)
administration (3)
advance (warning, etc.) (12)
advertisement (5)
afford to do something (17)
AGM (Annual General Meeting) (4)
analyse (the market, etc.) (21)
announce (19)
announcement (18)
apply for a job (20)
appoint (15)
appointment (6)
arrange (a meeting, etc.) (8)
assistant (2)
attend (a class, conference) (7)
average (14)

bankrupt (go bankrupt) (12)
bankruptcy (17)
board room (9)
boss (13)
branch (of a company) (2)
break (n) (between work) (6)
briefcase (13)
briefing (6)
brochure (12)
business administration (3)
business deal (13)

campaign (advertising) (6)
canteen (9)
career (20)
catalogue (2)

catering (21)
CEO (Chief Executive Officer) (4)
chairman (17)
chart (8)
c/o (care of) (4)
colleague (19)
company (1)
competition (competing firms) (8)
competitor (18)
complaint (21)
computer (1)
conference (1)
connect (a telephone, computer, etc.) (11)
contract (n) (11)
contractor (18)
corridor (9)
cost (n) (15)
course (of training) (3)
crate (2)
credit (n) (12)
current (situation, etc.) (7)
customer (12)
cut (in interest rates, etc.) (18)

day-release (course) (3)
deal personally with something (13)
deliver (2)
delivery (19)
department (7)
deputy (20)
design (v) (7)
design (n) (19)
desk (5)
develop (a product) (7)

development (in a situation) (12)
diary (of engagements, etc.) (19)
dimensions (of object) (5)
diploma (3)
directions (to a place) (9)
director (11)
disc drive (8)
discuss (5)
discussion (12)
display (n) (5)
division (of company) (2)
do business with someone (11)
drawing pin (10)
duty (particular job) (21)

economic (3)
economical (14)
economics (6)
EEC (European Economic Community) (4)
efficient (13)
electronic (13)
employee (2)
engaged (on telephone) (24)
engagement (business) (6)
equipment (11)
evidence (12)
executive (22)
exhibition (6)
expand (an expanding market) (4)
expense claim (7)
expensive (15)
expertise (12)
export (v) (3)

factory (2)
fall sharply (17)
fax (n) (9)
feature (of a piece of equipment) (5)
feedback (from customers) (23)
felt-tip pen (10)
fierce (competition) (15)
figure (number) (3)
file (business) (8)
filing cabinet (5)
fill in (claim, etc.) (7)
finance (n) (7)
financial (13)
firm (n) (2)
floppy disc (8)
folder (8)
forecast (n/v) (17)
founded in (year) (15)
foyer (of a building) (8)
freight container (5)

fuel (12)
fuel consumption (15)
future (6)

get in touch with (17)
goods (3)
government (13)
GMT (Greenwich Mean Time) (4)
graph (16)

head (of department) (21)
headquarters (9)
healthy (profits) (15)
high-quality (3)
highlighter pen (10)
hold a post (job) (20)

import (v) (3)
improve dramatically (13)
income tax (16)
inflation (15)
information (2)
innovative (15)
inquiry (2)
install (equipment) (11)
instalment (11)
interest rate (15)
interview (n) (20)
interviewer (21)
in-tray (18)
invest in something (15)
investment (17)
invoice (11)

job losses (18)

keyboard (8)

lecture (6)
leisure activity (16)
level (of training, etc.) (3)
liaise with someone (21)
line (telephone) (24)
load (of goods) (2)
loan (4)
location (8)
loss (not profit) (18)

mail-order (5)
mailshot (21)
major (repair, etc.) (8)
maintain (a machine, etc.) (7)
manager (4)
manual worker (2)

manufacture   (3)
market   (2)
marketing   (8)
market research   (19)
market share   (2)
MD (Managing Director)   (4)
measurements (of a product)   (5)
member (of an organisation)   (4)
message   (2)
microphone   (17)
microprocessor   (3)
model (of product or machine)   (7)
modern   (15)
monitor (n) (VDU)   (15)
monitor (v) (check)   (21)
mouse (computer)   (8)

name tag   (1)
nationality   (1)

on strike   (13)
order (for product)   (12)
overseas   (12)

PA (Personal Assistant)   (4)
pack (v)   (2)
package   (5)
paper clip   (10)
partner   (11)
pay cheque   (21)
pay demand   (13)
pay offer   (17)
pay talks   (17)
per cent   (2)
percentage   (2)
performance appraisal   (21)
performance (of a company or employee)   (15)
personnel   (9)
petrol   (12)
photocopier   (7)
photocopy   (9)
plan (n)   (19)
plan (v)   (2)
PLC (Public Limited Company)   (4)
pocket calculator   (5)
politics   (6)
post room (in a company)   (9)
post (n) (job)   (17)
postage stamps   (10)
poster   (7)
potential (customer, etc.)   (21)
printer (computer)   (8)
produce (v)   (3)
product   (2)

production   (7)
profitable   (4)
profits   (7)
progress (in training, etc.)   (21)
project (n)   (12)
promote (to a better job)   (18)
promotion (of a product)   (21)
proposal   (11)
PS (postscript)   (4)
publicity campaign   (14)
publicity   (12)
put up (increase)   (18)

qualification   (3)
quality   (15)
quantity   (12)
quotation (estimate)   (18)

rate (of tax, etc.)   (16)
R&D (Research and Development)   (9)
reasonable (price, etc.)   (15)
reception   (8)
receptionist   (9)
recommend   (10)
record (v) (payments, etc.)   (7)
recruit (staff)   (7)
recruitment (for jobs)   (21)
reduce (the workforce, etc.)   (15)
regional branch   (11)
reliability   (15)
reliable   (13)
rent (n)   (5)
reorganise   (13)
repair (n/v)   (8)
reply (v) (to a telephone call)   (8)
report (n)   (3)
report (v)   (11)
research (n)   (14)
reservation (hotel)   (19)
reserves (of oil, etc.)   (3)
resign   (13)
responsibility   (21)
results (for the year, etc.)   (15)
retire (from a job)   (18)
rise steeply (price, tax, etc.)   (18)
routine   (6)

sae (stamped addressed envelope)   (4)
safety   (18)
salary   (15)
sales manager   (2)
sales outlet   (2)
sales representative   (12)
sale (selling transaction)   (3)

schedule (6)
scotch tape (10)
section (of company) (14)
sector (of an economy) (3)
secretarial (9)
security (21)
seminar (6)
senior (adj) (20)
service (n) (3)
session (of discussion, etc.) (6)
sheet (of paper) (8)
showroom (8)
sign (v) (11)
software (11)
SOR (sale or return) (4)
spare capacity (12)
spare part (8)
specification (5)
speech (public address) (12)
staff (7)
staple (stationery) (10)
stationery (10)
stiff competition (17)
stock control (11)
store room (9)
subcontractor (12)
subsidiary (23)
supermarket chain (16)
supervisor (20)
supplier (7)
supply (v) (4)
switchboard (21)
system (11)

table (printed) (16)
takeover (2)
technical (23)
technician (12)

technique (of sales, manufacturing, etc.) (15)
telephone call (7)
telex (9)
timetable (6)
title (of talk, book, etc.) (19)
totally unacceptable (offer, etc.) (13)
tough (bargaining) (15)
trade exhibition (12)
trade fair (19)
trainee (7)
training (3)
transport (2)
trial run (of computer program, etc.) (18)
trip (business) (11)
truck (1)
tycoon (2)
type (v) (a letter, etc.) (7)
typing error (10)

unemployment (17)
up-to-date (15)
urgent (24)

value for money (5)
VAT (Value Added Tax) (4)
VDU (visual display unit) (4)
VIP (very important person) (4)

wage (18)
warehouse (2)
win (an order) (7)
work plan (8)
worker (3)
workforce (2)
workshop (teaching procedure) (6)

yearly (adj) (3)